FT Clark

63848

STFW-22OCT58-MINOR A/C
58- F100F 563848

284G-36TFW-22OCT58-MINOR A/C ACC
10 OCT 58- F100F

IDENTIFICATION CARD

Name FORREST FENN
Address 1413 N. Main St.
City Temple, Texas.
Phone 4303
Employed By
Serial Security No.

17	150	6'	Br.	Blue
AGE	WEIGHT	HEIGHT	HAIR	EYES

MONDAY
16 SEP
1936

The Thrill of the Chase

A Memoir

Published by ONE HORSE LAND & CATTLE CO.

P.O. Box 8174

Santa Fe, New Mexico 87504

First printing, 1,000 copies

All rights reserved

ISBN: 978-0-9670917-7-8

PHONE: 505.982.8520

EMAIL: ffenn@earthlink.net

Drawings by Allen Polt unless otherwise noted

EMAIL: polt@taonet.com

www.allenpolt.net

Treasure photographs by Addison Doty

The Thrill of the Chase

A Memoir

By Forrest Fenn

All of the stories that mingle among these pages are as true to history as one man can average out that truth, considering the fact that one of my natural instincts is to embellish just a little. Nevertheless, the story about my treasure chest is true, and if it doesn't stir your spirit then I hope at least it brings a smile in one of your dreams.

And please don't fret too much if some of the things I say don't appeal to you. Instead, keep in mind that the temperament of the country was different in the 1930s, when I was a tyke and Wimpy hamburgers were a nickel. If it will bother you to read that I shot meadowlarks so my family could have food on the table, then please don't read further. I did that more than once, and candor demands that I admit to being as proud of it today as my father was of me then, when I was eight. Please overlook my slight penchant for provocation and realize that all of us are environmentalists to some degree, and me more than most. My church is in the mountains and along the river bottoms where dreams and fantasies alike go to play.

Varied are the many roads I've travelled to reach my eighty years and not all have been paved with smiles and accolades. If to be content has been my goal then I've been successful my share of the time. But that's not to boast about all that happened along the way. Gaining experience wasn't always peaceful, especially during my early years of anxiety.

I tend to use some words that aren't in the dictionary, and others that are, I bend a little. My only goal in this endeavor is to talk about a few of my life experiences and if any readers over the age of twelve don't see a little of themselves in this mirror, then maybe they deserve another turn.

This book is my ninth in twenty-six years of casually recounting the things I enjoy most. My books have to write themselves or I struggle. This one did.

"Life is a game of poker,
Happiness is the pot.
Fate deals you four cards and a joker,
And you play whether you like it or not."

*This book is dedicated to
those who love the thrill of the chase.*

Well, I'm almost eighty and I think that's so funny. Oh, I don't mean it's funny because I'm almost eighty, but it's funny because I said it that way. I could have just said I'm seventy-nine so I could be a year younger, but I don't care anyway. Over the years more important things came in and out of my life so I never much cared even then. In younger days I didn't know where I wanted to go, but it always seemed kind of important at the time that I get there.

Then all of a sudden I started getting bald, just a little at first so it wasn't a big deal. I remembered that the same thing happened to President Eisenhower and he explained it was because his brains were pushing his hair out. I figured the same thing must be happening to me, so I felt all right with it. And then my hair turned grey – okay, white – but that problem was easily solved by just telling people I was dyeing it and they never knew the difference.

It doesn't matter much to me if I get old, especially since I'm already there. Actually, the only thing about me that's old is my body. My mind stays at about thirteen. To help my self-image I take showers only at night so I can't see my age as much. When my wife built our house, she put a skylight in my bathroom flat above the shower. It was a design deficiency but she didn't have to stand there and see so she didn't care.

Some people can live with old age. My dear friend Eric Sloane was a painter and writer of large note. When he got to seventy-nine like me he said it was okay. He wrote about fifty books and they were all clever. He always told me he was going to write one more book, title it *Eighty*, and then die. He was funny like that. Oh, I don't mean he was funny because he said he said he was going to die, but funny because he had all of that figured out. He said that his habit of never dating his letters or paintings was not a careless oversight, but rather a deep personal superstition that ignoring time itself might be a secret technique to delay aging. He probably thought that up when he was about fifteen. Later, in *Who's Who* he said his birth date was 1910 instead of 1905 and "hoped his friends would forgive him that foolish prank." I wish I could be clever like that. When he turned eighty he gave himself a surprise birthday party because he was surprised he'd lived that long. He died two weeks later while standing on a street corner in Manhattan waiting for the light to change. I'll never get over that. Who knows how long he might have lived if he hadn't had to wait for the light. Life is like that sometimes, and death is always too harsh.

Life for Eric was just a rule of thumb anyway and he was philosophical about it all. He was married five times, and he said he always married housekeepers because when he divorced they kept the house.

But being almost eighty gives me a lot of time to think about regrets and other things. "Who would you rather have working on your car, a man who just graduated from four years of mechanics school or a guy who has been working on broken cars for four years?" My father said that to me one day with no one else around. Can you believe that? He was just standing there by the car doing something important, and he said it to me out of the blue. He was really smart that way. We both knew I wasn't going to college, me because I didn't think I could make it, and him because he didn't think I could make it. I always listened closely when he talked and told me things. Sometimes he would ask me a really important question that I didn't know how to answer and make it seem all right. I'd just try to shake my head yes and no at the same time, but that was hard to do. Occasionally it's wise for the fox to dress like the hound. So mostly I just stood there and tried to look interested. ■

The author signing books
at the turquoise mine.

IMPORTANT LITERATURE

I still think about education sometimes, especially now that it's too late to get any. But with all of my days now, in the fullness of time, it seems prudent to do a little investigating about higher things. Because I wasn't in college I didn't get to read any of the great books that were written by really important writers, those guys like Hemingway and Fitzgerald, whom everyone looked up to. Maybe it's a respect thing, like the sheriff who told the outlaw he was going to hang him with a new rope because he respected him so much.

So one day when it was raining, I went to Border's to see about those books. I just wanted to look at one and hold it for a while. That's how old guys are you know. Maybe I should've stayed in school and studied more. History doesn't reveal the alternatives so I might've been a great writer for all I know, or even a great something better than that.

Just as I was about to ask the little girl at the computer about those authors, she raised her coffee cup to take a sip. And I swear that cup all but covered her whole face. I thought maybe she was trying to hide. Anyway, when she finished sipping she gave me a nice smile that made me feel better, and asked me to please follow her as she regaled me with the reasons why we are so lucky to have great books in our lives. I already knew that no salesperson has ever been accused of understatement so there was no reason for me to listen to her – but I did anyway.

That little lady probably knew where every book was in that whole store, and when we arrived at the exact spot she pulled down two books and just handed them to me and walked away, tossing her thick braids back and forth like they had purpose. She didn't even say goodbye or anything. But I noticed that she really felt proud because I could see it in her strut, and it was obvious that she'd graduated from a good school somewhere.

So now I'm holding copies of *For Whom the Bell Tolls* and *The Great Gatsby* and standing right in the middle of the entire book store with people all around. I didn't dare look to see who was staring, but finally, when I sneaked a peek, no one was watching. They were all just holding books and reading for free. To be a little candid, I thought it was rude of them to read with no thought of buying or anything. Stores have to make a living too.

The two books I held, that had such big reputations, were about six inches tall and four inches wide and really thin. I was so amazed that they were paperbacks. I didn't understand how two guys who were big shots could get by with writing such little books. I'd written eight books and all of them were much larger and cost a lot more money, and nobody has ever heard of me. If it hadn't been for the honor of the thing I'd have probably just put the books right back on the shelf and walked out. But everyone would have noticed, so I had to stand in the checkout line behind a bunch of middle-aged-looking people. Most of them were women because I suppose all the middle-aged-looking guys were at work someplace, or doing something else. I don't think they go to bookstores much.

Well, you could almost guess how slow the dumb line was moving. The only register guy in the place was showing more patience than

I felt at that moment, while two borderline biddies were preoccupied with some kind of breathtaking nonsense at the expense of my time and patience. Finally they selected a couple of impulse oddments and the line started moving again. It was hard not to think of what people have to go through when they get old. It doesn't matter that teenagers have to stand in line for hours because they have so much time left, but for old guys who are pretty much covered up with their lives already, it's a different story. Life can be so rude that way.

When I got around to reading that bell tolls book I thought it was just plain. The story was about this guy who was an ambulance driver in World War I and he was in love with a nurse. There was lots of killing and mud and bombs and dead horses. I read about a third of that thing and couldn't force myself any longer. Who did this Hemingway guy think he was anyway? I didn't think his book was even sort of good. And what made it worse was that the Gatsby thing wasn't much better. Those two writers were so overrated I couldn't believe it. I could've been embarrassed for both of them if I'd thought it'd help. But the college professors always assigned these books – so there certainly was that to think about.

Finally, I just tossed those beauties in the trash basket under my desk and looked away. If Robert Redford had ever written anything he probably could have done it better than the guy who wrote that Gatsby book.

Not having gone to college began to take on a whole new meaning to me now and I was reinforced in the belief that I had hardly missed anything. Besides, some of the things I do pretty good I'm better at than some of those college guys are at what they do pretty good.

Well, as fate would make it happen, the very next morning all the news was about this guy J. D. Salinger who had just died.

Everyone on the TV was talking about how he had revolutionized writing novels in his day, and so on. The news said he was very secretive about what he did, and even Diane Sawyer mentioned that he'd written a lot of books and had hidden some in a vault so no one could read them. He seemed like my kind of guy but I couldn't figure out how he could be such an important writer when I'd never even heard of him.

At Borders the next day it was still raining so I just wandered around the store. I didn't spend much time in the children's section or cooking or travel. Finally, I found the area I was looking for and pulled out *Catcher in the Rye*. It was an average looking book about the size of the two I'd thrown in the trash, but it seemed better to me because I didn't expect much from it.

So I strolled over to the check-out guy who probably remembered me from the day before. When I handed him the book and my credit card he said in a loud voice, "*Catcher in the Rye.*" That idiot! So now everyone in the whole dumb store started staring at me and not at him. He's the one that said it, not me, but that didn't make any difference. Some women were sniffering and others were just grinning. It was all so rude that I just looked away. That taught them.

The loudmouth check-out guy thought what he'd done was real clever. He probably was on something and I don't think it was Ovaltine. He just stood there making his six-bucks-fifty an hour and picking on elderly gentlemen such as myself. Don't you just hate guys like that? I've never been able to find a place where I couldn't embarrass myself and this store was now number one on the list.

Well, the first sentence read "If you really want to hear about it, the first thing you'll probably want to know is where I was born, and what my lousy childhood was like, and how my parents were occupied and all before they had me, and all that Copperfield kind of crap, but I don't feel like going into it if you want to know the truth." I thought what a great way to start a book – just get right down into the fling of it. So I read some more and then some more, and then I read the whole book. The story was about this guy who wandered around the streets in Manhattan a lot, had been thrown out of a few schools, and thought his classmates were idiots. And then you know what? The more I thought about it the more I realized the book was about me, and I couldn't believe it. How would anyone imagine a coincidence like that could happen? Admittedly the places in JD's book were different from mine and the names were different and the time was different from mine, and the schools I never heard about were obviously different, but other than that it was my very own story line. He even had a sister like mine, the guy in the story I mean, not JD. And it was so funny, and I mean really funny because I always thought I'd write that book myself. Only I'd have put a lot more in it, like things I did in school, some of which would not be too complimentary. That's why I was going to call it an unauthorized autobiography, if that's the right word. What do you think? But I'd have to tell everything straight because nothing is worse than facts written wrong. Just because Napoleon said that history was nothing more than fables agreed upon, doesn't mean it's true.

Actually, there were two reasons why I never got around to writing my book. One was because I always had other important things to do, and making plans is antagonistic to freedom. But the other reason was more important; my self confidence was really down at the bottom. A kid I didn't like at all had given me a copy of *Kismet* to read, and he probably did it on purpose. The story was about this poet in Baghdad who was always picking some guy's pocket, and he was in trouble most of the time, the pick-pocket guy I mean.

Anyway, there's this line in the story: "To the Caliph I am dirt, but to the dirt I am a Caliph." Well, you know he had to be an educated guy to say something that good. But how would you like it if someone said you were dirt? Life is so unfair and people are always doing those things. I probably would still be down if JD had not insinuated that I should write my autobiography.

So I started to figure things out. Einstein said, "Imagination is more important than knowledge," and I had a lot of that, imagination I mean. Besides, non-fiction writers don't have to be right but eighty-five percent of the time and everyone knows that. How else can a person write a book? I never thought I had to believe everything I said and if I had to look up a word I just wouldn't use it. And because I'm so easily pleased, a lot of things are effortless for me. I had it all figured out. So when *Catcher in the Rye* was done I threw it in the trash where it landed right on top of a *Time Magazine*. I just needed some time to think, and the more I thought about JD the more I liked him. The only thing was, he'd left out some really important stuff about when I was a kid and doing different things. Maybe he just had it in mind that I'd finish the book, or at least add on to it. So I reached in the trash for *Catcher* and put it on my desk so everyone could see that I'd read it. I think my friend JD knows. And in a serious, determined way, I started to think about what to say.

Not a day passes that I don't question myself about what lies just ahead and whether or not I can make it happen like it's supposed to be. Now, near the end of my seventy-ninth year, each day tests me in a different way and I know that before too long I'll make my last flight to where even memory itself will never have been. Sooner or later each of us will be nothing but the leftovers of history or an asterisk in a book that was never written. So now I sit here past midnight, beside my juniper fire, reflecting back to the year when my awareness took its first few steps. *

FIRST GRADE

MONDAY
16 SEP
1936

My father was a teacher at Lanier School when I started first grade and after a couple of years he became the principal. His promotion was a really big deal because he got his own parking spot in front near the door where he went in. I remember standing there while he hammered the wooden sign into the ground, "Mr. Fenn, Principal."

But I can't say the sign didn't make a difference in my life because it did. No one else had a sign so it was easy to notice and I used to point it out to all the kids. There was this one guy, John Charles whatever, who didn't like me or the sign much. He told my friend Billy Joe Ray that he was going to beat up on me just so he could see how high I'd bounce. Sometimes John Charles would bring a little jar of green olives to school and wave that thing in my face. Can you imagine that? It was one of those long thin jars with a green lid and the olives looked like they were placed in there one at a time. What was that all about anyway? But he was having a tough life and I kind of felt sorry for him. His mother used really bad language on him and she didn't even care who was standing around with big ears. I mean it was *really* bad language and it ticked off my father pretty good when he heard her say some of those things to her kid. I guess she never understood the

Mr. Fenn, Principal

irony of calling him a son-of-a bitch.

My father talked sometimes about another old lunch-bucket woman. Her name was Ora Mae and I knew her a little from the halls. She seemed happy enough with her way of barely getting by, but she was always hiding out and smoking cigarettes with no names on them. Being the school janitor was a big deal and I suppose that's what she was. She mostly just did odd things and cleaned. She was a little critical of our school's organization and sometimes mentioned things to the kids. My dad stopped liking her when she said that he was nothing but a cheap, one pony show. I never knew what that meant but it must have been really bad because it made my father mad. And my mother always took his side so that was two against one. Everyone knew that my mother wasn't much in a fight, though. My father always said she wouldn't bite a hard biscuit if she was starving to death. That made her laugh. ■

ME   EDARD   PAT

Lanier School,
Temple, Texas, 1936.
My father is standing
at the far right.

KACIR   SKIPPY

NO PLACE FOR BIDDIES

Lots of people are always saying that youth shouldn't be wasted on the young. What a stupid thing to say. Of course youth should be wasted on the young. That's when kids start to be noticed as real people instead of just babies. For instance, I remember when I was about eight and overheard two ladies talking. They were neighbors who lived down the block, and both thought they were better than me because they lived in a brick house. One said to the other, talking about me of course, "He'd run away from home but he's not allowed to cross the street," and they laughed real hard and didn't even care who heard. How humiliating do you think that was for a kid my age? And sure enough, it had to happen at the big church social when absolutely everyone was there. Well, I didn't say anything out loud at the time but I certainly remembered, and I've loathed those old biddies ever since. They were a lot older than me, probably at least thirty, and both were married although I can't imagine how they put that together. How intimate they were with their husbands is probably a matter of academic dispute anyway because the tall one was the best excuse I can think of for zero population growth.

Besides, I could cross the dumb street anytime I wanted to and it was stupid of them to say I couldn't. I walked to school almost every day didn't I? And cars were whizzing every which way weren't they? But just to be safe, my mother always told me to wear clean underwear in case there was an accident. She was smart like that and I usually did what she said because I loved her so much. She was a perfect example of nature's long-sightedness and everyone around our block knew it. And just to prove the point, when I walked to school I always watched where I put my feet on the sidewalk. "Step on a crack and break your mother's back." I always remembered that one, and that's why my mother was so proud of me.

And as far as running away from home was concerned, no kids ever did that back then because they just didn't. Those things came later when girls started making trouble. Anyway, those two old biddies are probably long since dead and what do I care? That'll teach those two. ■

SUNDAY
2 SEP
1943

That's me at age thirteen,
thinking about starting seventh grade.

JUMP-STARTING THE LEARNING CURVE

In 1943 I started the seventh grade in junior high school where my father was the newly appointed principal. It was there that my life really began, but for the first ten years I figured that if it weren't for my name I wouldn't have anything at all. Then, when I became a teenager, things just got worse. The good part was that I wasn't even smart enough to know I wasn't very bright, until one day my teacher asked, "Forrest Fenn, don't you know anything?" I replied, "Miss Ford, I don't even suspect anything." Then for some strange reason, what I had just said seemed to take on a purpose of its own. It was a primeval thought but maybe it made me think deeper down. No matter what I lacked or lost, bad grades and all, they couldn't take away my name.

What caused Miss Ford to focus on me in the first place was that I always sat in the back of the room where I thought she couldn't tell whether I was asleep or not. My perceived detachment had developed into a cat-and-mouse match of sorts. So one day she asked the class a question and called on me to answer. To everyone's surprise I answered correctly and that startled her pretty good. She said to me, with that sideways-looking face, "Forrest, were you asleep?" I said "No, Miss Ford, I was awake." "Well, your eyes were closed," she said. "No, Miss Ford, my eyes were open; it was just my eyelids that were closed." I said that to her as gently as I could and quickly crossed my legs. The snickers around the class did little to belay her anguish and just for a faint moment, my growing aware- ness compared the look on her face to a can opener ad I'd seen in *Good Housekeeping Magazine*. Anyway, I was ahead for now, but I remembered what I'd heard once on the Amos 'n Andy radio show: "Don't make the alligator mad until you've crossed the river." All of the bravery was in my talk and I knew that sooner or later I was gonna get mine. Fortunately the bell rang about that time and I was out of there like a cannon ball on fire.

Now, I secretly loved that old lady Ford, and I say old because she had to be at least forty. She was barely pretty but hadn't yet gone to seed and I suspected that she had a lot of woman left in her. Her problem was that she kept trying to teach me Spanish by talking Spanish all the time. I never figured out that technique. Besides, other important things were building up in my mind. I had so many thoughts I could hardly keep them in my mouth.

So when some of them got out one cloudy day Miss Ford grabbed my arm in a huff and marched me down to my father's office. I had seen her mad before, but not like this. She wouldn't look at me, but I could see her face. I always thought that if you left things alone maybe they'd go away, but not this time. I knew I was about to enter personality rehab. Her mouth was moving in fast cadence with her choppy steps and it was obvious that rage had found a home.

My dad was sitting at his desk doing something very important when she blurted out, "Mr. Fenn, your son called me an old bat." Well, my education was fast approaching graduation with that one. He looked a little corroded and suggested that Miss Ford leave "and please close the door behind you." About that time my father gave me a look and I mean *really* a look. I was sure a window pane somewhere in Mississippi was about to break. Just as he started to lean into some pretty strong adjectives, I quickly held up my hand and interrupted. "Father," I said, "her story isn't exactly right. What I said was 'my father says you're an old bat.'" He slowed to a stop as my words began to soak in and I could see his mood changing right there in front of me. He remembered when she'd called in sick one morning and he had to leave the breakfast table to find a substitute, and the telephone was clear down at the end of the house. He really hated that, especially since the biscuits and gravy were hot on his plate.

Now his demeanor was one of deep compassion and under-standing. He rested on that for a moment, then he sat down, twisted his chair and took my hand. "Okay son, what have we learned from all of this?" Well, I didn't have a clue about what we'd learned, but

was praying thanks to Thor because he was holding my hand and smiling. My father I mean. "What we've learned is that you should always tell the truth, but you should not always tell ALL of the truth." Boy oh boy, those five minutes were better than all the diplomas in Texas. I had just learned about fear, hate, ethics, dread, moralities, passion, honesty, subterfuge, truth and a bunch of other things I can't even remember anymore.

I prayed for D's in all of my classes, but no one ever listened. So I decided to just do things my own way and to heck with what people thought. If they weren't paying my bills, I didn't have to listen to them, unless they were saying something I wanted to hear, of course. My father was paying my bills so I had to listen to him.

Anyway, I figured my failing classroom grades were more than offset by my valedictorian marks in Savvy 101 and Street Smarts 102. My father once told me, "The greater part of knowledge is knowing those things not worthy of knowing." Now why would he tell me something like that? He just said it right out. Was he trying to justify my lack of ability to take a test? Maybe he was thinking that if I could just somehow get by in life I'd be way ahead.

One day my father gave me a spanking at school for running across some stupid desks, then that night he gave me a spanking at home because I got a spanking at school. The more I thought about that the more I felt put upon. When I explained to him that I'd been double jeopardized he told me that those things didn't count in a dictatorship. That's when I first started to mistrust governments.

It was easy to justify the time I spent in Spanish class looking out of the big window that was adjacent to my desk. It was on the second floor, and a beautiful old iron, slide-down fire escape was just outside that window. When the sun was out, the smell of freedom was more than I could resist. So on occasion, when Miss Ford was writing Spanish words on the blackboard, I'd quickly slip through the window and down and away. I was proud to have thought of that idea all by myself. I remember the exhilarating feeling that there were probably a lot more ideas out there that were just as good as that one.

Fortunately, I was the only one in the class who knew that trick, the sliding I mean, and even though that rusty old iron thing marked the tail of my britches pretty good with a heavy brown color, it was worth it. Everyone who walked behind me on the way to the next class knew what I'd done. People were beginning to notice me.

To Miss Ford, out the window meant out of sight where I couldn't cause her any trouble. She was going to flunk me anyway, so what difference did it make? I was beginning to learn where the edges were, and later in life it would come to me that one of the greatest mistakes of human endeavor has been the belief that wealth and fame could always equate with intelligence. ■

Central Junior High School. The wonderful iron fire escape slide is on the back of the building — 1943

That's my father in the back,
    brother Skippy on the left, sister June on the right
and me and Bessie in the middle — 1937

BESSIE AND ME

My father got a Guernsey calf that grew up to be a beautiful fawn-colored animal. We called her Bessie. I loved that old cow and it was fun to milk her before school and again before supper. She liked me so much she'd swing her tail as a sign of friendship, and to swat flies. But what had once been a very effective fly-swatter soon became so dog-chewed on the end that there was nothing left but a hard knot. It looked terrible, but she couldn't see it and I tried not to look. I usually tied it to a fence post before I started milking because sometimes she'd give a hard swish, and club me on the head. It hurt plenty, and if I flinched too much I'd either fall off the stool or kick the bucket over trying to get out of the way.

All the cats in the neighborhood knew when I was in the barn and would come running. It was so funny. All six of them would just sit there like wet socks hanging on a clothes line, waiting their turn. I gave each cat about five squirts, and although I had pretty good aim, sometimes I'd miss their mouths a little and splatter them in the face instead. They didn't seem to care much about that and when it was over they'd walk away licking themselves and feeling blessed.

One cold morning when Bessie was further in the barn, over

That's Me and Skippy in front
with neighbor kids — 1932

near her stall, I thought it would be all right to just tie her tail to one of the legs on my milking stool. My thinking was that she couldn't club me if I was sitting on the stool. But there must have been some big flies around because she swished that tail so hard the stool went flying, making me fall into a fresh cow pie. Until you have loved a cow, part of your soul remains undiscovered. Miss Ford suggested that next time maybe I should change pants before class, and it was just like her to say something like that. If she'd known I was running late for school she might not have said anything. Sometimes teachers just don't understand. ■

The Fenns — 1935

MY SPANISH TOY FACTORY

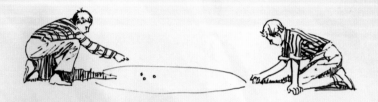

Like most kids my age, I was always hungry, but I didn't like to take a brown bag to school. There was just something about a dry sardine sandwich and a noisy apple that didn't appeal to me, so I spent most of my class time grinding marbles. Playing marbles at recess was a big deal in 1943. If I could find a good-looking rock, during the next hour I could grind it against a small sandstone slab that I always carried in my pocket. By the end of Spanish class, I had a pretty round marble that I could easily sell to one of the rich kids who always had a ride to school. It didn't hurt much that I was the Grand Marble Champion of the seventh grade in Central Junior High. I made sure that all the girls knew about it.

The going rate for one of my marbles was a dime. I could feel between my knees where to grind to make it round so I could keep my eyes on Miss Ford. She thought I was paying attention and that always made her suspicious, and I think it affected her concentration some. As sure as anything, that dime could get me a bag of Fritos and a Coke, and to me a lunch didn't get much better than that.

After awhile I began to think bigger and started whittling yo-yos and spinning-tops during class. For those wooden beauties I could get a quarter, and that meant two bags of Fritos, a Coke and a small ice cream, leaving me a nickel as a head start for the next day.

I was beginning to learn the value of money and the advantages of a capitalistic system of government. Although it may not look like much now, it was a big deal to me then. My father was probably a little proud and although I wasn't getting much education I was sure getting experience. Any part of some is better than no part of any. I was beginning to like myself.

When I walked the mile to school on cold mornings, my path took me right past the pie factory on First Street and French. It was hot inside by the stoves, so a giant fan would blow the aroma of fried pineapple pies right out there on the sidewalk in front of me. I remember the beautiful, old, gray-haired lady who did the cooking. The price of a pineapple pie was a nickel, or two for a nickel if they were broken. Well, when I'd open the back door to that place during the lunch break and walk in, that sweet old lady would see me coming. She knew I didn't have any money so she'd break two pies. I still remember that grandmotherly look on her face and I've thought about her in some of my best dreams. If I could find where she's buried I'd slip out there some dark night and push a nickel under her grave marker and just leave it there. Somehow I sense she knows that and is smiling down on me. ■

SATURDAY
10 JUL

Father & Mother

June, Me & Skippy at Hebgen Lake
floating on a log

ME IN THE MIDDLE

Our family was probably a lot like most other families, only better. My maternal grandmother, Arie Beatrice Simpson, used to tell me about when she was a little girl growing up in Ft. Worth. In those days, the Comanches would sometimes run through the family's barnyard trying to catch chickens. She'd stay inside the house with her nose pressed against the window and watch. The Indians really had fun, sometimes running into each other in the chase and falling down laughing. The hens were kept busy flying and cackling and flopping around, losing feathers while trying to get away. It was so funny, but probably not for the poor chickens.

My mother, Lillie Simpson Fenn, also grew up in Ft. Worth but by then most of the wild Indians were gone. She met my father when he was attending TCU and they were married in 1926. My brother Skippy came along two years later, then it was my turn, followed by my little sister June. There were two years between me and both of them so I was in the middle and that was significant because I felt somehow surrounded. You can laugh at that if you want to, but think of it this way: Skippy was older so I looked up to him, and June was younger but I couldn't look down to her because my father wouldn't allow it. Does that seem fair? My siblings are gone now and so are my parents. It sure would be nice if they could all come back so I could be in the middle again. ∎

TEMPLE, TEXAS

Me and June
playing Billy the kid.

SURVIVING MYSELF

I always thought getting out of bed in the morning was cruel and unusual punishment and I hated it with a passionate fervor. But I slept in a room next to the kitchen so the smell of bacon and eggs in the skillet could prompt some movement. Bessie was always up early and I had to milk her before I could eat. My parents were smart that way.

Breakfast in our family was always homemade. We churned our own butter, gathered eggs from the chicken barn, butchered our own hogs and put mom's specially preserved jellies and jams on the biscuits.

In those days the noon meal was called dinner, and we had meat only on Sunday after church. Dad usually killed a chicken and Skippy and I would pluck the feathers, which was really hard. We experimented dipping the dead thing in scalding water first, and that helped a little, but the smell was terrible. Finally we'd just grab a bunch of feathers and jerk as best we could. Mom was world-class at frying chicken and my sister June always helped. We were a close family, and everyone but mom and dad pitched in with doing the dishes. And my brother Skippy of course. He always had some urgent calling elsewhere.

My father gave me a Daisy Air Rifle for my eighth birthday and I used to shoot it all the time. I even taped magazine pictures to the wall in my room and shot at people, usually guys who were wearing black hats. I pretended to be Hopalong Cassidy.

On Saturdays I'd go out behind our house to shoot meadowlarks for supper. The front sight on my gun was a little crooked so I had to off-set some when I aimed, but that didn't matter because I knew exactly how much to the side I had to point. I needed to get five birds, one for each member of the family, and sometimes if I couldn't find but four meadowlarks, I'd shoot a scissortail as a replacement. The trouble with robins was that they could see the BB coming and duck, so I learned not to waste shots on those guys.

Scissortails were smaller but had long tail feathers and were a different color, so if I had to settle for one of them I'd always take the feathers off before I got home so no one would know what it was. And I'd track it through the cleaning, cooking, and serving process because I had to make sure that June or Skippy got that one. I figured they wouldn't know the difference, but mom and dad sure would, and I didn't want it because scissortails ate some pretty disgusting things. Since I brought the food home I was higher on the food chain than my siblings. At least it was fun thinking that way.

Sometimes during supper mom would ask us what we wanted for dessert. I always said strawberry shortcake, Skippy would say he wanted pineapple upside-down cake, and June liked something else. So mom would trim the edges off of several slices of homemade bread and then cut the pieces into fourths. When they came brown out of the oven, she'd put butter and different kinds of homemade jams on each piece, and serve them hot. Boy! We always made a big deal out of taking a bite and saying, "ummmm, mom, great strawberry shortcake," and "ummmm, mom, great pineapple upside-down cake." I can still remember how much my dessert tasted just like what I asked for, and in my fantasy way, it was.

When "Mr. District Attorney" was over at 8:00 o'clock, the kids had to start for bed and that ritual was set in concrete. On really cold nights father lit the gas stove in the sitting room because that's where the night radio was, and the whole family huddled around it. The rest of the house remained cold, and my room didn't even

Skippy & Silver

June & Silver

have a stove. But the second the minute hand touched 8:00, father would give us a few seconds to warm our pillows and that was it. June always ran straight to bed and mom would tuck her in, but sometimes I'd watch Skippy to see what he was going to do. My father never knew what the word bluff meant so he'd just sit there and give Skippy about five seconds of additional parole time. And if there was no movement, we both got spankings without a word being spoken. How's that for motivational training?

Father liked Skippy best and I knew when he got a licking anything could happen after that. So I'd just stand there and wait for my turn at the paddle. Mom was always knitting and didn't seem to notice, and June was asleep by that time, so it never became an issue in the family. After four or five times the spankings began to work for me, but I'm not sure Skippy ever learned; maybe he was turning Alpha.

June never got switched because she probably did everything right. She was the family pet, being both female and the youngest and all. I remember one time I made her so mad she kicked at me as hard as she could. I saw it coming and quickly turned my foot sideways, which made her shin catch the full impact of my cowboy boot and it really hurt her. Father gave me a spanking for that. I suppose I should have let her just kick me in my shin. If there'd been time to think and I could've weighed the difference between being kicked by my little sister and getting switched by my father, I probably would've taken the switching again. Sometimes principle is reason enough to abandon logic, no matter how much it hurts.

June usually hung out in the kitchen with mother and listened to "Your Hit Parade" on the radio while preparing supper. It came on at 6:00 on Saturday night and was seriously suspenseful for them. The ten most-asked-for songs of the week were played, starting at the bottom. As the crescendo built everyone guessed which song would be number one. Many times I'd win and it made everyone mad because I didn't much care one way or the other. Skippy never participated because he was above such nonsense. He was a lot like my father.

Sometimes, when it wasn't too cold, I'd get even with my father for switching me by jumping out of the window by my bed and walking down to the cemetery, which was just a block north of our house. It took guts to go in there when it was dark with no moon. I still remember the sense of accomplishment I felt when I sat on some dead guy's grave marker. I wasn't even afraid. A kid really has time to think in a graveyard. ∎

GYPSY MAGIC

42

In the spring when the weather was warm, I used to raise the window that was at the side of my bed and put my pillow on the sill. I slept that way whenever I could. The Katy railroad tracks were about a half-mile from our house and late at night I could hear the steam engines puff and the engineers blow their air horns. It was a soothing sound and sometimes I think I can still hear it when the wind is out of the east.

The gypsies came through town several times a year in their horse-pulled wagons that had rubber tires. They camped down by the tracks in a big circle. At night they built a large fire in the middle and five or six girls of all ages danced around it, their hands swishing long skirts back and forth to the beat of Cajun accordions and harmonica music. Some of the men played fiddles.

If my head was in the window I could hear the sound and instantly knew what it was. The screen was easy to unlatch so I'd jump to the ground and run as fast as I could through the cemetery and across a wide field toward the firelight. By lying on my stomach under a wagon, and pushing the tall grass aside, I could really see up close. The flashing flames made dancing shadows that seemed to move with the music, and there were times when I thought the girls saw me as they swirled by, but no one said anything. I touched them with my eyes and became part of it as I moved back and forth in the sway. I always stayed until the fire died down and the music stopped. But sometimes I still hear it in my dreams. ∎

The Main Street Cowboys

3 JUN

1930s

Carl & Arie Simpson
and the grandkids

OFFICE

Helping Father
make fire wood

IN LOVE
WITH YELLOWSTONE

My dad had the summers off, being in the school business, so that meant for three months I didn't have to worry about taking a test or having to please Miss Ford. Father would load our '36 Chevy up to the top and we'd take off for Yellowstone. I absolutely loved that place and along the rivers I could find the best agate rocks for making marbles. I was thinking about all of those things and even more.

You may not be old enough to know that a war was going on then and that everything was rationed: tires, gas and lots of other stuff. So we drove 35 miles an hour for 1,600 miles with no air conditioning or radio. Even so, my father always drove about 50 miles out of our way, down a little dirt road to a one-room school house in Wyoming, just to show me what was written over the door. "He Who Teaches a Child Labors with God in His Workshop." He was so proud about that.

Then my father sold our '36 Chevy and got a '41 Plymouth instead. I couldn't understand how he could do that to such a faithful car that had been a member of the family like the rest of us. How would you like to be replaced by a newer model? I felt very insecure for a long time after that. If he'd get rid of that car maybe he could get rid of me too. If I could find that Chevy I'd buy it back and keep it forever. ∎

WEDNESDAY 13 JUL 1955

My one-room cabin in paradise,
with curtains on the windows
but no heat, no water and no plumbing.

The paperboy

THE TOTEM CAFÉ CAPER

One summer I found myself selling newspapers on the streets of West Yellowstone, Montana: *The Montana Standard* and *The Billings Gazette*. That was many years before the streets were paved, so the deep potholes on Canyon Street often were filled with water that was fair game for every car that bounced by. I think they competed to see which one could splash dirty water on the most people. I used to hide behind a tree and laugh.

Anyway, I made a penny for every paper I sold and it soon added up pretty good. But the sack my eighty pound body had to carry was so heavy it was tiring even to think about it. One morning I sat down to rest on the curb in front of Scaggs Grocery Store when my boss just happened to drive by in his big, beautiful yellow Cadillac. He rolled the window down and yelled, "You're canned." That's all he said as he drove away! There was nothing not to like about him because he was so suave and all. I didn't really know what "canned" meant but guessed it must be something good because he was such a nice guy. When my mother told me I'd been fired I just stood there while the sun went behind a cloud. It killed me for sure, getting fired I mean, and all of a sudden I saw my stupid ex-boss for what he really was — a fat, baldheaded, hulk of a dirty name. I think his brain must have been constructed by the lowest bidder.

Now I was not only out of a job, I also felt like I'd fallen back to a place where there was no more back to fall back to. My mom said it was all right to cry so we did that while standing under the lean-to where my father kept the Plymouth. Maybe that's why she helped get me a dishwashing job at the Totem Café. The job was a big deal, right there in the best part of town on the main drag – well, it wasn't much of a drag, just about five blocks. Anyway, it meant getting up at 4:45 am to be on the job at 5:00 am and sixteen hours later my shift ended and I was eight bucks richer. Each dish and pan had to be washed by hand, dipped in scalding water and dried. Whew! My hands turned white and had deep canyons in them. What I really hated to wash were the giant kettles used for making brown gravy. The smell truly assaulted my sensitivities and that's why I don't eat brown gravy anymore.

But there was a wonderful old lady who also worked there. We called her Grandma and she made cherry and apple pies that smelled pretty good. One day, during the lull between breakfast and lunch, I apprehended one of her hot pies, tip-toed it out back behind a pine tree and ate the whole thing. When Frosty caught me there was a severe scene. Well, he wasn't even the boss; he was just the manager, but he was pretty full of homage for his own person and everyone around there knew it. One day Grandma took me in the frozen meat locker and said that when the owner gave Frosty an inch he thought he'd become a ruler, Frosty I mean. Anyway, Grandma told the guy that she'd given me the dumb pie and it was her right because she'd made it on her break. And I added that I had just borrowed it. The Ruler thought both excuses were pretty lame and he fired me right there in the dessert section of the cafe. He said I'd stolen the pie without his permission and he was going to dock my pay. I didn't have a clue about what that meant but I noticed that no one was clapping.

While I was drying my eyes the waitress was standing over behind the far counter. "Who's gonna wash the dishes? Not me!" she yelled. Well, Frosty started wheezing and making funny sounds, kind of like a garbage truck does when it backs up, and he just stood there for a while like he was trying to figure out the secret of thought. When he finally spoke, his voice was a few octaves higher than before and it made me wonder a little about his polarity. But it didn't make any difference to me. What he did when he was off duty was his business and I wasn't about to make an issue of it, especially with the whole staff watching. But he finally capitulated, saying that I had misapprehended what he meant by the phrase "GET OUT," and reminded me that I was still hired in fine standing, and the dishes were piling up. Somehow I wasn't too flattered, but anyway – I won't mention anything more about that pie caper except to say that the precedent had been set and I grew to really love Grandma. We got to be a pretty good team, especially on Frosty's day off. ■

MY BROTHER BEING SKIPPY

My brother, Skippy, was always doing things that I thought were both atrocious and astonishing. He was kind of a god to me. In Temple, when he was fourteen, he built a helicopter-looking thing using a washing machine motor for power. He worked on it after school and on weekends, and wouldn't let anyone help. Finally, when it was time for a test flight folks gathered in our front yard from blocks around. Skippy fiddled around with last minute adjustments then climbed in the seat. The crowd was hushed, and when the engine started everyone backed up and some of the girls covered their eyes.

Well, the rotor blades started turning, slowly at first, then faster and faster until the whole machine rolled over on its side and parts started flying through the sky like missiles. Most of the crowd fled the scene, and my mother said it looked like a Chinese fire drill. When Skippy crawled out of the wreckage my father and I rushed up to congratulate him on his accomplishment. We were so proud because someone swore that the flying machine had actually lifted an inch or so off of the ground. Skippy later said, "What did you expect for free admission?" He was like that, and then was off to another adventure.

He never lost his inventiveness or his originality, and was the most intuitive person I ever knew. One summer, when he was still

FRIDAY
5 JUN 1413

Skippy on high school graduation day.
You can see that he hated all four things: the hat,
the tie, the smock and the event. Father was proud.

MY BROTHER BEING SKIPPY

a teenager, he disappeared into Idaho for a couple of days. Then one morning he called and asked us to go out to Hebgen Lake because he was flying in and was going to land on the water. Never mind that he didn't graduate from flying school.

Hebgen Lake was huge, but because it was 6,000 feet above sea level no one ever landed on it. Well, sure enough, in about thirty minutes here came Skippy in a two-seated, pontoon airplane that made so much noise it must have scared the fish for miles around. After circling around a few times for maximum effect, and to every-one's bewilderment, he landed right in front of the dock. His big grin told us nothing, but also everything.

The problem was that the plane couldn't take off again because of the altitude, and I don't think Skippy even cared. We sure had fun gassing the throttle and splashing around that poor lake trying to get airborne. One of the men fishing over near Watkins Creek was a pilot. He told us that if we couldn't get that machine in the air in fifteen miles of water runway we should just give up. The family thinks Skippy took the wings off and trucked the plane back to Idaho where it belonged. Skippy never would say, of course. ■

SUNDAY
23 MAY
1940s

Skippy

THE LONG RIDE HOME

One fall, when it was time to go back to school, Skippy got an old Model B Ford and announced that he was going to drive it home to Temple. The fact that he didn't have a driver's license didn't seem to be a consideration. It was just 1,600 miles across five states. Father said he couldn't go by himself so I volunteered to go along and ride shotgun. That surprised everyone, including me and Skippy.

So off we went at twenty miles an hour and with almost no money. We had a flat about every 50 miles so the car was packed with spare tires that we had salvaged from city dumps along the way. The war was on and tires were hard to come by. Both of us were still young enough to know everything, he more than me because it was his car and I was just his passenger.

That trip was really educational for us. We counted the antelope and ducks and chipmunks, and the many unknown furry things in the road that had been run over so flat that the ravens could hardly pick up the parts. Sometimes Skippy would slow the throttle to five miles an hour so we both could get out and run alongside the car. We did that for miles, and occasionally he'd jump on the running board and turn the steering wheel a little to stay on the road.

In Wyoming, between Shoshoni and Casper, we had some kind of slight misunderstanding and I told him to just stop the dumb car and let me out. To my utter amazement he did, and then drove away. It was on a long, straight stretch of road with no cars or people around anywhere. It was so far away I don't think they even had coyotes out there. I watched him putt-putt over a distant hill and disappear while I just stood there with an incredulous look on my face. It seemed that I had become a detriment to myself.

I had no money, no coat, and no shoes. I remember sitting down beside the road for about an hour to consider my lot in life

Skippy holding a rock

and ponder if anything was left of my future. No cars passed and it was getting cold, so I started walking on the paved road in my socks. After another hour or so, off in the far distance, I saw Skippy coming back for me. I didn't think he would and neither of us said a word. I just crawled in and we drove off. I loved him forever after that and we never fought again. Sometimes it's good to just slam the door on a relationship and start over.

Looking back now, after almost sixty-five years, I have fond memories of that road trip. Skippy died in a scuba diving accident in Cozumel, where they found him in ninety feet of water with his weights on. His luck failed him in the end and it didn't surprise me at all. At age fifty, he was plucked from life at the moment of his greatest blossom, and I knew he wouldn't go in any normal or mundane way. I had to bribe two Mexican officials to get him home. Skippy had such potential and there were so many things he would have accomplished. We should have buried him standing up. ■

Me & Lightning

LOOKING FOR
LEWIS AND CLARK

A few years later, when I was sixteen, I read a book titled *Journal of a Trapper* by Osborne Russell, who travelled along the Madison River in 1835, just outside of West Yellowstone where Hebgen Lake is now. Russell, along with a few of Jim Bridger's trappers, was attacked by eighty Blackfeet Indians near where Hebgen Dam would be built nearly a century later. After a brief fight, Russell escaped west toward Stinking Creek. About thirty years earlier, Lewis and Clark, on their wonderful Corps of Discovery, had passed through Montana not too many miles to the north. I was thrilled and wished I could have been part of those great adventures. Sixteen-year-old kids are like that I guess.

Anyway, after telling my parents that my elbow needed some room, I mentioned to my friend, Donnie Joe, that I was going out to look for Lewis and Clark. He was quick to take the hint and said he would just ride along and help me keep the mountains company. So we rented a couple of horses from a friend and started up Red Canyon. Why my horse was named Lightning was something I never figured out because he hardly had the power to get out of his own way. As it was important to be honest with the situation, we limited ourselves to three Babe Ruth candy bars each, bedrolls, a shotgun, fly rods, knives and matches. And we got a map of the

Gallatin National Forest that would really come in handy later on.

The first afternoon we found ourselves way up on top of a beautiful mountain under a lapis lazuli sky. We were thrilled and knew the whole place was there just for us. Surely the rippling brooks would be grateful for our company and the grizzlies would understand that we were just exploring the area and meant no harm.

Well, the first night we couldn't get the dumb fire started, and we had already used most of our matches, so we very wisely wadded the map and hoped that we would be forgiven that one small foible. It worked and as the fire crackled and our horses wandered off, we ate our three candy bars and talked long into the night. Osborne Russell had been in those mountains for nine years and suddenly we felt like we were with him.

We spent the next day looking for the horses and finally found them down by a rivulet where the grass was tall and abundant. There were no fish around anywhere and prudence whispered that we should not shoot the two magpies we saw. Later we realized the folly of that decision.

The next day we rode the mountains, the hills, the valleys, the hollows, the dales and the depressions, looking for something to catch or shoot. There was almost nothing, but we did shoot one animal that I promised not to talk about. So on the fourth, fifth, or sixth day, I forget which, we were pretty sure we'd used up most of the fun.

I could have tolerated Donnie's displeasures more easily if my saddle sores had not become such an issue. The insides of my legs were raw most of the way down. I found that riding behind the saddle on Lightning's warm, soft, furry, rump helped some but he didn't like it much and kept doing some funny dance step that I didn't trust completely, so I put my handkerchief over the hardest part of the saddle and tried to think soft thoughts.

But Donnie got in a serious swivet and wouldn't speak to me for a while, except to say that our unfortunate adventure was ill-conceived, dumb thought out, and I was over-rated like my horse. I think he even compared my intelligence unfavorably with that of the two of us, the horse I mean. He said that he had important things to do in town and insisted that we go out. I quickly agreed, but the problem was neither of us knew where out was.

So I applied some mountain man wisdom to the situation. The sun comes up in the east and we thought out was south so that made it easy, except that south was over the highest mountain we'd ever seen. It didn't help much that a bunch of arrogant ravens kept flying around yawking at us, and always out of range. They probably knew that our hunger had long ago stopped being just a theory.

Donnie started to look like an untipped waiter and when he leaned a little forward in his saddle and just stared at me, I knew enough to be still and watch the trees, after I took this photograph.

We decided to follow a fast-running stream that seemed to have an anxious purpose of some sort. At least we could have water and surely it would lead us to a road or a Forest Service man-trail somewhere. Gradually, that little stream got narrower and narrower and deeper and deeper until it developed vertical sides that nothing could get through but water. I think Donnie was getting delirious because he kept saying, "If we don't change course soon we'll end up where we're going."

Then his right stirrup strap broke and he had to ride on one foot. Well, that was it. He got real serious about being mad and lost at the same time. He insinuated that I couldn't find my butt with both hands and all the lights on. When Lightning seemed to take his side I knew the crisis had arrived. So we turned back for half a day until we found another stream to follow. Bad luck can always be trusted.

I won't dwell further on that because I'm grateful that the space between fact and fiction is often blurred by the passage of time, except to say that we finally loosened our grip on the reins and the horses took us to a dirt road. We were 50 miles from where we started and Donnie was in good spirits again, and started talking coherently. He's gone now, but I still think about him a lot. At the time, we were both important to ourselves in our own way, and for the same reasons, but no one will judge us anymore when I'm gone too.

A few days later with the luxury of hot chocolate, I made some notes that might be helpful to any future sixteen-year-old geniuses who think looking for Lewis and Clark might be fun:

• Hunger is both unrelenting and unreasonable.

• You can't hide from thunderstorms.

• Porcupine meat tastes like kerosene.

• Coffee made by boiling pine needles can bring on cardiac arrest.

• There's nothing worse than a wet bedroll on a cold night.

• Mountains can suffer instant personality reversals.

• The older you get the smarter your parents become.

• Movies lie to you.

Over the years I've read *Journal of a Trapper* a dozen times, and always with a deeper appreciation for who Osborne Russell was and what he did. The mountains continue to beckon to me. They always will. ■

Skippy in his car; the grin is real.

June & Donnie in Skippy's car before the windshield fell off.

BUFFALO COWBOYS

Skippy had an old car with no top; it had one big seat in the front and that's all. One day, when a buffalo wandered out of Yellowstone Park and started tearing up fences, Donnie Joe thought we should go out and round it up. So after loading Skippy's heavy boat-anchor rope in the car, the three of us went looking for the buffalo. We found it about seven miles west of town in a large, sagebrush flat that had stands of pine trees everywhere. He was a big bull and we started calling him Cody.

After a quick vote they decided that I would be the one to catch the buffalo, so after tying one end of the rope securely to the front axle of the car, I started my stalk. Big buffalo bulls have no enemies so it was easy to slip up behind a tree and throw a loop, which landed on Cody's head and wrapped around both horns. I slowly inched the rope tight, then retreated about fifty feet to the car. Skippy and Donnie were in the front seat grinning. I sat on a sofa pad in the back and held on to the car frame, wondering what we were going to do next.

Cody didn't even know what had happened and just kept on eating, so Skippy honked the horn a few times, and that didn't matter either. One time the bull looked at us with total disinterest, but when he grazed to the end of the rope he knew something was funny and started making new rules. At first he just jerked his head from side to side, and then he jumped up and down a few times. We decided later that they must have been warm-up exercises. Our car started to maneuver a little because the slack was gone from the rope.

Then all of a sudden Cody decided on a change of venue and started running. It wasn't a fast run because he was pulling a car loaded with three guys who were about to learn the folly of their adventure. When Cody panicked and started snorting as he ran, we suddenly realized that buffalo bulls are easier to grab hold of than they are to turn loose of. I thought about bailing out of the car, and probably would have if I'd had my shoes on.

Skippy was steering, trying to dodge trees and stay behind Cody, because if the car turned away something unfunny would

Cody resting

probably happen to us. Finally we dropped about a foot straight down into a stream of fast-moving water, and when we got to the other side the car stopped with a terrible jolt. Skippy and Donnie flew over the dashboard and I was thrown onto the front seat. The engine was in the water and the fan was throwing sprays all over the place and making noises like a helicopter.

It took us a few seconds to recover and realize that the axle and both front wheels had gone with Cody. When last we saw him he was still running and the tires were bouncing wildly like some circus acrobat.

I lost my shoes in the ordeal, Skippy lost his car and Donnie lost his credibility. The long walk home was wet and cold, and we didn't realize until much later how fun it had been. Cody was found and shot, and his meat was made into buffalo burgers at the Stagecoach Inn. It made me really mad so I never ate there again. ∎

Me & Donnie with a prize catch
from Grayling Creek

STOUT-HEARTED MEN

When my Yellowstone summers were over I was a nineteen-year-old lank without discipline, focus or cause. But I knew it was time to get serious about something because my potential was about to burst inside of me.

Many of my high school buddies were preparing to go to Texas A&M and I felt left out. It was a transitional time for me and I wasn't taking it too well. At the last minute I asked the gang to come by and pick me up so I could go along. I didn't want to go to college; I just wanted to be with my friends.

Since I'd not registered, the school didn't know I was coming, so I just checked in and was issued a cadet uniform like everyone else. Whatever classes my buddies attended, that's where I also went. I even took some notes so I would look legitimate.

A&M was an all-male school at that time and they had a great plan for promoting instant camaraderie that kept most of the homesick kids on campus. They put heavy doses of saltpeter in the food and built huge bonfires at night so the cadets could herd in close and sing songs like the one Romberg wrote:

Give me some men who are stout-hearted men,
Who will fight for the right they adore,
Start me with ten who are stout-hearted men,
And I'll soon give you ten thousand more.
Shoulder to shoulder and bolder and bolder,
They grow as they go to the fore.
Then there's nothing in the world can halt or mar a plan,
When stout-hearted men can stick together man to man.

I loved it beyond description and suddenly everyone was a friend to be trusted. How could they not be? And then after about four days, when we were playing touch-football, my name was called over the loud speaker. "Cadet Fenn, report to finance." I knew my college education had ended so I hurried back to my barracks, packed my extra shirt and tooth brush in a brown paper sack, left my beautiful cadet uniform folded on my bed, and headed out the back door. To avoid detection I ran full speed across an open field, crying all the way, until I reached a small county road that led back home. I remember falling twice while trying to get through the dumb barbed wire fence.

After trying to thumb a ride for a few minutes I saw an A&M pickup truck make a turn and come my way. When the driver asked me what was going on I said I was headed home because there was no money for me to stay. Those were magic words and he could see that I was distraught all over myself. Without comment, he turned his truck around and drove away. I think he was one of the stout-hearted men.

The little county farm-to-market roads in that area were short and had many intersections, and it wasn't easy catching a ride in the direction I needed to go, so that night I slept under a tree with cows grazing all around. It was a threshold moment in my life, but I didn't know it at the time. ■

SATURDAY 27 DEC 1953

TUY HOA, S. VIETNAM

Peggy modeling
her swimsuit

High school sweethearts

Our wedding,
Dec. 27, 1953

MY WAR FOR ME

The Korean War had started three months earlier so I joined the Air Force as a private and was sent to radar mechanics school in Biloxi. A big, ugly, sergeant gave me purpose for the first time in my life and it wasn't very funny. Sometimes just lasting something out can be a triumph. To get away I volunteered for everything I could find in the manuals. Fortunately, they needed pilots and I was accepted into training.

The problem was that I was in love with the most beautiful girl you could find anywhere. Peggy Jean Proctor was her name and we had been dating for a few years. She was in Houston going to college and I was traveling all over the countryside trying to learn to fly airplanes. Everyone knew that she was too good for me but tenacity was never one of my shortcomings, if you know what I mean. Graduation from pilot training was in September and we were married after she got her degree, three months later. I had plush assignments and my wife was always by my side.

In my first fighter squadron I flew the F-86D, which held the world's speed record at the time.

I learned to fly in the T-6, which was the hardest airplane in the world to land — 1953

Aide-de-Camp to
Major General Frank H. Robinson,
1955.

1958

In Germany my squadron flew the F-100C and
I sat alert with an atomic bomb under my wing.

Then as a general's aide I flew most of the later fighters and even went to helicopter school. In Germany my squadron flew the F-100C and I sat alert with an atomic bomb under my wing. The world was tense, but for us life was good and our first daughter was born.

After a few years, an unfortunate conflict started in Southeast Asia and I was separated from my wife and two beautiful young daughters for a year. I was reminded of what my dear friend and Texas patriot-historian, Evetts Haley, said of his wife Nita. It is so beautiful and fitting that only my lack of eloquence and articulacy could have prevented the words from also being mine. If Evetts were here, surely he would allow me the fantasy pleasure of addressing them to my wife as well:

> Courage wears a crimson coat
>
> Trimmed in trappings bold;
>
> Knowledge dons a dress of note,
>
> Fame's cloth is gold.
>
> Far they range and fair they roam
>
> Much they do and dare,
>
> While gray-gowned patience sits at home,
>
> And weaves the cloth they wear.

What follows is something I did write. Its sudden arrival on paper should not be confused with how long it took to get there. Some stories must move at their own pace and in their own time. This is one of them.

When the Vietnam War came along, I found myself a fighter pilot major in the Air Force. All the frailties of humankind had manifested themselves in that beautiful place and that terrible situation. Lyndon Johnson had summed it up under the heading of "Saving South Vietnam and all of Southeast Asia from Communist Aggression." I bought into that pretty good. All the pilots did. The endless hours of classroom training and sorties flown on the gunnery ranges around the world had bred us to it. It was almost umbilical. How faint it seems to me now and how dreadful it still must be for so many others.

After all of the bullets and rockets and bombs had finished flying through the trees and across the skies, there was nothing left for us but the memory of 58,266 Americans whose names have been etched, chronologically by time of death, on that shiny black war memorial, which is constantly being washed clean by the tears of a million visitors. In another generation or so most of those names will be but an asterisk in the history of a forgotten war, a curiosity to wonder about, like the Lincoln Memorial. How unfortunate it is that world leaders are constantly bringing war and death to those of us who are doomed to follow their dictates.

Later-elected officials will all ask the same question and give the same answer: "Why?" and "Never again." Of course they don't know why, and there will always be another again. Almost 2,500 years ago, Plato said that only the dead will know the end of war.

I didn't pay much of a price in Vietnam and I feel a little guilty for that. Perhaps I was spared to tell a tranquil story that unfolded

I climbed that ladder 274 times in Vietnam and each time I wondered if that beautiful plane would bring me home again. It did — 272 times.

upon me without a scar or even a bad dream, but has provided a profundity of emotions that still dwell deep and resonate inside of me, almost like a missed heartbeat. And I am coming to that.

Many professional soldiers who have been in the throes of life-or-death experiences may be forever branded by an incident, although it may have lasted only a minute or two. Later, in one's reverie, those memories can come sparking back when ignited by something innocently said or something thought. If you see a warrior staring off, quietly move away.

So it is with me now, as I sit here past midnight, alone with only myself to know. I remember how it was at Tuy Hoa on the South China Sea in South Vietnam. Everyone was nervous on their first mission into dangerous air, and I was no exception. But this was somehow different. I had flown 326 combat missions and had been shot down once already. This mission was scheduled to be my last because my year was almost up. The "freedom plane" was to take me home in just four days, on the 24th of December, 1968.

Some weeks earlier our F-100 single-seat fighters had flown eight ship sorties into North Vietnam where the dangerous air lived in great abundance. I could feel it beaconing me to come and see, and I embraced the thought. Air Force F-105 fighters from Korat, Udorn and Ubon, Thailand had flown hundreds of missions in the north, and those pilots were all heroes to me. The F-100 Misty forward air controllers flying out of Phu Cat, South Vietnam, were just as brave and the Hanoi Hilton was full of them.

Our Operations Officer was relaxed and cavalier in his briefing: "Don't worry about the friendlies – there aren't any up there. Pick targets of opportunity on the way back if you have Mic-Mic (bullets) left, but don't make a second pass. Keep your airspeed up. If you get in trouble, go for the water squawking Mayday. You guys are seasoned

After taking off from Tuy Hoa
we headed north.

in the soil and I'm not worried." Yeah, right, he wasn't going.

A few minutes later we were in position and ready to roll.
With a hand signal to my wingman, we slowly moved our throttles
forward to the stop and we held the brakes hard. A quick scan of
the twenty-four gauges on the instrument panel said my ship was
willing and ready, so with a head nod we rolled in tight formation.
After three more seconds and another nod, we each moved our
throttles outboard to the afterburner latch. Then, with only a second's
pause, the fun started as 16,000 pounds of thrust and fire exploded
from our tailpipes through silver-plated titanium eyelids that quickly
moved in and out, then settled on an optimum temperature that
gave maximum power. At lift-off the predictable whisper of the

afterburner was soothing and reassuring, and we soon outran the sound. My F-100D was so solid and strong that being afraid wasn't easy. But with four 750-pound bombs, 600 rounds of 20mm, high-explosive incendiary bullets, and 550 gallons of fuel in two high-drag external tanks, we weren't exactly charging the sky. The climb out was smooth as usual and the jungle through my windscreen was a deep green and covered with trees 300-feet high that seemed less and less important as we clawed for altitude.

To the right was the beautiful South China Sea that I had known for many months. The green was different from the color of the trees, but just as beautiful. In a way that I can't explain, the sea seemed somehow foreboding and sinister, at times even diabolical. Maybe it was because I knew the history of that water, its treachery; it had diluted the blood of so many sailors who had dared to test its beauty.

At about 4,000 feet I jiggled my rudder pedals, signaling my wingman to move out so he could relax and we could better keep the watch. Suddenly, something wonderfully innocent occurred. A small clearing appeared at eleven o'clock on my canopy and slowly worked its way under my left wing to disappear behind. It was magical because a small waterfall in the center of the clearing dropped water so far that it turned to mist before it could spread on the rocks below. It must have been 100 feet or more. Large birds were circling around as if they also thought it was an amazing sight. How peaceful it all seemed.

I remember smiling and telling myself, in an idle whim, "If I get back from this mission, I'm going down there." It was a silly thing and I knew it, but the seriousness of what lay ahead that day somehow turned the whim into a vow, a pledge of sorts. I felt I'd made a deal with that beautiful place. "You bring me back and I'll come down there and personally thank you." The deal was struck.

I trusted it and it could trust me. It was our secret alone.

All of our planes returned from that mission, and we kept going back. On each successive climb-out, before the clearing could disappear beneath my wing, I winked and renewed the vow. And I kept returning.

On one mission in North Vietnam, after dropping bombs and turning for home, I let down to 1,000 feet looking for targets of opportunity, maybe army trucks or a munitions storage area. My wingman was 1,000 feet on my right and back at thirty degrees. At twelve miles a minute the geography was changing fast and my brain was thinking and planning minutes ahead.

Suddenly, on the left there appeared a large group of people bunched together, maybe a thousand or more. I wasn't ready for what was about to happen. Although my guns were hot, I knew I wasn't going to shoot because I had to first determine if it was a

At Cung Son, South Vietnam. When "off duty" I flew a number of missions with Forward Air Controllers like Dan Harshman.

legitimate target. If it was, I couldn't come back around for a strafing pass. It was too dangerous. What I could do, though, was call the guys behind me and give them the coordinates.

So with an alert to my wingman, we turned in and started down to 500 feet and lit the afterburners. When I got to the edge of the crowd, I rolled on my left wing to get a good look.

It was a funeral!!!

We were traveling so fast no one had heard us coming and when I rolled my wing down I could see nothing but panic and yelling and screaming and stampeding and terrible fear. It was horrible. Women were running with babies in their arms; children had started fleeing in every direction with their arms up as if they were surrendering. One old, bearded man with two walking sticks just looked at me as if he were resolved to meet his fate.

I was so ashamed I started crying in my oxygen mask. Sobbing. I could hardly see through the dark visor on my helmet and the salty tears burned my eyes in a way I had not known for a long time. Suddenly, I hated Lyndon Johnson and Robert McNamara and all of the other politicians who were sitting in their fat offices at home, totally oblivious to what war was really like.

On the first of November, 1968, all flying in the north stopped and we started bombing in South Vietnam again and in Laos, which was also dangerous air. President Johnson, who was now maneuvering for peace, was telling everyone at home that we weren't bombing the Ho Chi Minh Trail in Laos, but no one told us we weren't.

About six weeks later, on the 20th of December, three wingmen and I took off for a serious target at Tchepone, Laos (Chapone to us). Both the Air Force and the Navy had lost planes on that target in the previous days, and the intelligence officer who briefed us on the mission didn't tell any jokes as he was supposed to.

After takeoff we rendezvoused with a KC-135 tanker, topped off our fuel tanks, and headed for the target. Each of our four F-100s was loaded with different ordnance. My plane carried four CBU-34, which the Defense Department designated as "Aerial Denial Bomblets." We were going to mine the main road on the Ho Chi Minh Trail. The plan called for me to go in first while my wingmen held high. I was to drop bomblets on each of two passes.

It was 1755 (5:55 PM) when I ejected from my crippled F-100 and floated down into an uncertain environment. I closed my eyes tight as my body crashed into the trees, breaking limbs that bounced me around for what seemed like an unreasonable length of time. It didn't help that the wind-blast during ejection had jerked the helmet off of my head. Finally, my descent was broken when the parachute tangled in a tree, and I felt myself gently bouncing up and down for a few seconds. When I opened my eyes I was eighteen inches above the jungle floor and I couldn't believe my good fortune. I quickly unfastened the parachute harness and stepped to the ground.

Eighteen days earlier I'd been shot down near Binh Thuy in the delta region of South Vietnam, and it taught me that bad luck is not something that always happens to the other guy. I thought that any landing I could walk away from was a good one. The incident at Binh Thuy taught me that some landings I could limp away from were also good. When in combat, even if there was chaos all around me, there was always a feeling of tranquility that came from the firm belief that I was totally invincible.

But at Chapone, the instant it became evident that my airplane wasn't going to take me home, every feeling I had seemed to have a mind of its own. There was no panic or heightened sense of anxiety, but my brain shifted into an adrenalin overdrive. Confidence can only come with knowledge and training, although a good ego helps.

Every night during my year in Vietnam, the last thing I thought of before going to sleep was my bailout procedure. It was burned into my brain: remove the film from the gun camera and zip it in my G-suit pocket, put the cord of my Minox camera around my left wrist and pull it tight, throw my tape recorder on the floor, stow all loose gear, fasten the chin strap on my helmet and lower the visor, put heels in the ejection seat stirrups, force head back against the headrest, straighten back, lift the arm rests to blow the canopy, pull both ejection triggers.

And if the emergency didn't allow the seven seconds it took to complete the whole procedure, then go directly to the last five, because failure to do even one was usually disastrous. Broken necks, backs and legs were not uncommon.

My canopy had been shattered by gunfire, but large, jagged pieces of thick plastic were still attached to the aluminum framework just above my head. I worried that the ejection seat mechanism might have been damaged, meaning I would have to crawl over the side and manually pull the ripcord of my parachute. I needed some luck. When I lifted my arm rests the canopy frame blew away from the aircraft as advertised and I felt better. Although the jungle was dense I decided to continue my descent and wait until the last second to eject. I didn't want to be shot in the parachute. When I reached what I thought was 1,000 feet above the trees I pulled both ejection triggers.

What followed was a blur of activity. I was blown from the plane by a 37mm cannon that was designed to provide seat clearance over the vertical tail when traveling at high speed. Then a rocket ignited automatically, propelling me up another 150 feet, while two nylon straps behind my back reeled in, throwing me from the seat, which fell away.

37 MM ROCKETS

JAN 1968

Survival School in
the Philippines with
Negrito Pygmies.

Tiger skin
nine feet long,
Cung Son Special
Forces Camp,
South Vietnam.

When my parachute opened I remember being surprised by the sudden silence, although it made me suspicious. As pre-planned, I took pictures of the blossomed parachute above me, the jungle through my boots below me and the plane before it crashed. It had about four and a half tons of fuel on board and I was watching when it hit half way up a 1,000-foot-high stone bluff. The fireball was huge and I knew it would attract unwanted attention.

Initially, I felt myself going into shock; I was clammy, hot, nervous. Then I remembered what they taught in "Snake School" in the Philippines. "One hundred percent of those shot down will go into shock and it can kill you. Lie down, elevate your feet to get blood to your head, think tranquil thoughts." So I thought about being with my father on the Lampasas River in Texas with a bobber in the water, catching five-inch bluegills. In thirty minutes I had recovered and felt strong and confident. And then I remembered the clearing and the beautiful waterfall. It was a stupid thought, but strangely tranquilizing. I felt like I would soon be going home and I laughed at myself for being so human. Attempts to contact my wingmen by radio were unsuccessful but the locator beacon in my parachute should have activated automatically. I knew my friends were listening for it.

Darkness comes fast in the jungle, and the night served a chilling menu of exciting events, the memories of which have both entertained and humbled me over the years since. I have a strong recollection of sitting on a damp, mossy log, wondering what to do next. I knew the Pathet Lao didn't take prisoners, so when I heard dogs barking in the distance, I quickly opened a large can of pepper that had been zipped in my G-suit for almost a year. After moving a few feet into a particularly dense part of the jungle, I spread the pepper in a circle around me, hoping to deaden the noses of any dogs that might get curious. Because the Air Force didn't issue pepper as survival equipment, a lot of the pilots made midnight requisitions at the mess hall.

The Laotian night jungle was a bustle of activity. Small animals constantly made digging noises, and there was a lot of loud squawking. I couldn't decide if those sounds were made by birds or monkeys. It might have been amusing if I'd not known that both cobras and tigers were also around. It was common to see their skins stretched on the tin roofs at Special Forces camps.

About midnight there was a bright flash of light that I estimated to be just a short distance away. I figured the air rescue guys were dropping parachute flares hoping to recover me before the enemy arrived. Then I experienced what was perhaps the most terrifying event of my life. The giant trees bent over and limbs broke as a shock wave of wind and noise blasted me to my core. The high bluffs behind me magnified the sound, and I thought my lungs might collapse. The roar was so traumatic I felt that if it happened again I might not survive.

I had experienced the effects of Operation Arc Light. Three B-52 bombers from Guam, flying in formation at 30,000 feet, had dropped 750-pound bombs. Each plane carried 105 such devices and they were being released one at a time but in rapid succession. The blast of noise continued for what seemed like forever. Three or four minutes after it stopped I recovered some of my senses. The jungle was strangely quiet except for the sounds of rocks and debris that began to land in the trees and fall around me. One small pebble hit my leg and I kept it as a souvenir to remind me of why I never saw any generals on the front line.

The B-52s came to see me again several hours later but I was ready. When I saw the first flash I hunkered down behind a log and tightened up as best I could. Nevertheless, I am convinced that thousands of animals, human and otherwise, were killed in Vietnam by sound alone.

At first light, I was making notes about what had happened. This is what I wrote while sitting under a forest of 300-foot-high trees that were covered with white orchids as far up as I could see.

"Made first pass 250° into the sun, 200', 500 knots airspeed, trying to surprise. Probably got hit on that pass. At the end of the run I whifferdilled up and to the right and back out of the sun hoping to blind the guns I knew were there. Expended inboard CBU-34. Near the end of the pass I got hit by probably 10 ZPU (50 caliber machine guns tied together and firing with one trigger) shooting from the side of a hill about 2,000' on the left and level with me. Hits in nose, both drop tanks, canopy shot off plus some in aft section because I got immediate compressor stalls and the oil pressure started down. (I pulled around abruptly and turned all four gun switches on so I could mark the guns that shot me. My 20mm bullets were incendiary and had explosive warheads, the blasts from which were lethal up to twenty feet.) Then headed 030° for bailout and instructed wingmen to hit, with all ordnance, the guys that had hit me." Later, one of my wingmen, Lt. Gary Van Valin, said something to the effect that, "I saw the guys shooting at you and I got them."

Although my engine had flamed out, with my remaining airspeed I had been able to get about thirty miles away from the target area and make it to a peaceful-looking part of the jungle. Later that morning, at 7:55, Lt. James Swisher, the forward air controller who had directed my flight the night before, came looking for me. (From seven miles away he had been the first to say I was on fire.) With the help of my little radio we were united, and he told me to hang tough, that he would be back, and then he left. Well, I remember thinking I'd just as soon he would hang around for a while. But he had work to do and within a few minutes the sky was full of American war planes, all intent on doing things that were in my best interest. I really love those guys.

While the "Sandy" propeller driven fighters strafed the jungle all around to keep the enemy heads down, two Jolly Green Giant helicopters arrived. My rescue was being coordinated by a Crown C-130 aircraft circling at 15,000 feet. The pick-up chopper came in low while the stand-by waited high in case it was needed.

The 240-foot cable ride up on a heavy, iron jungle penetrator through a tangle of breaking limbs, leaves, and tree trunks, took my breath away. When I reached the hovering helicopter, Flight Engineer Master Sergeant Maples had his left hand on the "Guillotine," a cable-cutting device that would have allowed him to chop my line if the plane started taking battle damage or if I had somehow become irretrievably wrapped around a tree, endangering the helicopter and the crew. But instead, when I reached the top, A/1C Robert Sully grabbed the hoist and swung me in the door. "Quick, get in the back and sit on a flak vest," he yelled. He didn't have to say it twice.

As the helicopter sped up and away I started taking inventory. Both my face and head were bleeding in a few places but nothing serious. My left shoulder ached and my arms and legs, although bruised, were intact. My pistol and Minox camera were gone from my body but my folding hat was still in my G-suit pocket. Every-thing considered, it was a great ride.

An hour later we landed at Nakhon Phanom, Thailand, where we were greeted by a couple of generals and a camera crew. I was the 1500th airman to be rescued by the Air Rescue Service in Southeast Asia. It was a noteworthy milestone for them and a humbling honor for me.

The next day, while climbing out in a C-130 and heading back to my home base at Tuy Hoa, the pilot asked me if I wanted to talk with my wife. So with patches through Saigon, Guam, and Barry Goldwater in Scottsdale, to Lubbock, Texas, Peggy and I spoke and said foolish things while everyone listened. She had received a telegram saying I had been shot down and "no parachute had been seen."

When we landed at my home base at Tuy Hoa, I told my boss that I didn't want to be shot down on my last mission and begged for one more. Every pilot's dread is to be shot down on his first mission, or his last, and when the latter happens it's a terrible bust on the morale of those remaining. A four-star general in Saigon gave his blessing saying, "…but keep him in South Vietnam."

After that mission, it was time to pay my debt to the waterfall and the magic clearing to which I felt so obligated. After some strong begging, an army helicopter-flying friend agreed to take me. It was about an hour's flight to where the little stream dropped so mistfully onto the rocks below.

When we landed, the geography looked much different from what I expected and from what I had seen from a mile up. The small clearing was now about 300 feet across, and belly-high grass made walking difficult. It was impersonal and disappointing. I was embarrassed and felt foolish for making such a big deal out of something that now seemed whimsical. Besides, this was enemy country, and although it seemed remote, we didn't know who might be nearby. Helicopters make a lot of noise so we agreed to stay only five minutes.

After sitting on the edge of the waterfall and throwing rocks over the drop, the pilot said, "Let's go." The sound of the rushing water was stronger than the noise of the idling engine and I was a little uncomfortable with the whole episode. As we rose and started walking in the tall grass toward the helicopter, a strange chain of

After being hoisted out of the Laotian Jungle and returned to friendly territory at Nakhon Phonom, Thailand, it was time to give some thanks. In the center is Lt. Col. John Carlson, who led a flight of four fighters and strafed around my position on the ground to keep enemy heads down. The helicopter pilot, Lt. Cmdr. Lance Eagan, shakes my hand while we all grin and rehash the rescue mission. They showed their strength when I needed it the most. How do you thank guys like that?

The "survivor" on the left (me) and the men who extracted me from the deep
jungle in Laos. They are all heroes many times over, as is the Jolly Green Giant
helicopter behind. Her name is the Candy Ann. From left to right: Lt. Col. John
Carlson – Sandy lead; Lt. James Jamerson – Sandy 4; Lt. Col. John H.l. Morse –
Commander of the rescue unit and co-pilot of the Candy Ann; A/1C Robert J.
Sully, the Parachute Jumper who pulled me into the helicopter: Lt. Cmdr. Lance
Eagan – pilot of the Candy Ann; Flight Engineer M/Sgt. Lee R. Maples,
who had his hand on the cable cutter.

events began to unfold. I tripped over something and fell flat on my face. That never happens to me. Then, when I started to push myself up, I came nose-to-nose with a rude aluminum grave marker. How strange and out of place it seemed.

I could barely read the dirty nameplate, but did make out the name of a French soldier. Then suddenly we saw more grave markers. The more we looked, the more we found. These soldiers had evidently been killed during the French Indochina war in 1947. But I had tripped over a crudely-made stone grave marker that had fallen face down in the grass. Before I could roll it over to see what it said, the pilot was strapping in. I had to hurry. A French name and rank was followed by arcing English words across the top:

IF YOU SHOULD EVER THINK OF ME
WHEN I HAVE PASSED THIS VALE,
AND WISH TO PLEASE MY GHOST,
FORGIVE A SINNER AND SMILE AT A HOMELY GIRL

Those words burned in my brain and I can see them just as clearly now as I did then, when I was so rushed. I took care to replace the stone marker as it had fallen, and smooth the grass to hide it over. The promise that place had made to me had been kept, and mine to it as well.

How innocent and foolish all of that seemed at the time, and even more so, that a strangely insidious something began to gnaw on me. This could not be the end of it. There was no feeling of closure at all, no sense of completeness. It was disappointing.

Is it fair that no one recalls where those brave French soldiers fell and are now interred in that remote jungle clearing, hidden from life for a million sunsets? After a violent ending, they have been swallowed up in a serenely beautiful place, and at the same time, hidden by the ravages of time and nature. Those who fell there, in that hateful, wasteful, losing war (like the one in which I was involved) are forever forgotten, save by me. It has been fifty-six years since that war, and no one cries anymore. That thought is deeply personal and indelible in me even now, forty-two years after I was there.

My experience beside the waterfall was on December 22, 1968. Two nights later I walked in my front door in Lubbock to be greeted by my lovely wife and two beautiful daughters. It was Christmas Eve.

For the next month, while I was on leave, the flourish of activities related to homecoming and reuniting with family and friends put my jungle thoughts on hold, except for occasional flashes that insinuated something unfinished. I didn't know enough about

what had happened to even speak of, much less understand, what I was feeling and what it could possibly mean, if anything. It took weeks to digest as thoughts slowly started to seep back. What was this all about? Was it nothing?

It was all a blur in my mind, like a dream that kept floating in and out. Before the war started, I didn't even know where Vietnam was, or Southeast Asia for that matter. It was so unlikely that I would be a fighter pilot and fly to that place. Why did the strange clearing mean so much to me? Why did I survive 328 combat missions but get shot down twice? Was it only to be drawn to that place? What kind of fool would take a defenseless helicopter to that waterfall? It was more than strange that I would fall to the ground and read such a poignant inscription. And why did the words impact me so? I had a lot to think about.

As the months passed and I got back into the swing of Air Force life, which by then involved teaching other men to fly, my thoughts naturally started to analyze the things that had hitherto been but a blur of incoherent incidents.

Then one day in 1969, as I was looking through my Flight Log, my eyes fixed on an entry that had only a brief explanation. But I knew! I remembered every detail of that flight and why I had marked it like that.

That flight had been many years before – thirteen to be exact – on the 13th of July, 1956. I had taken an old T-33 jet trainer from Stephenville, Newfoundland, to Pope Field, North Carolina. A party at the Officer's Club in Stephenville had detained me longer than I wanted, and although I was not a drinker, my body was already tired.

At about midnight I lifted off for a long, dark flight that would take me down the length of the Eastern Seaboard, across a blur of lights that never slept: Boston, Providence, Hartford, New York,

Philadelphia, Baltimore, Washington, Norfolk, and on. Because of the great distance involved, it was necessary to climb as high as possible – 49,000 feet – to save fuel. (Blood will bubble in the human body if pressurization is lost at 50,000 feet unless the pilot is wearing a pressure suit.)

I knew I was pushing it and the plane's oxygen system was antiquated. But the rules of flight were not unknown to me, and I was a careful pilot. On the left side of the forward panel, near the bottom, was a blinker. When I inhaled, the gauge winked, meaning I was getting oxygen through my mask. With a cockpit pressure altitude of 38,000 feet, I needed all I could get. The last thing the crew chief did after he pulled the chocks for taxi was to cup his nose with one hand and give me a thumbs-up with the other. That meant "Check the blink and good luck." So I checked the blink every few seconds of the flight.

After a long climb to level off and cruise, I felt myself trying to go to sleep. Flying the plane at that altitude was difficult enough without that kind of problem. I remember the air was quiet, even over the large populated areas. No one was around; no one was on the radio, no one to talk to. The impersonal lights were there, but I was all alone.

In order to stay awake I started playing stupid games, like moving my helmet from left to right then back and lightly tapping the canopy on both sides. That helped, but it was distracting and I didn't want to break anything. Finally I started moving my left hand in and out, looking at my glove as if I had not seen it before. Then, and for no reason at all, I closed my fist, stuck my thumb out, and moved it close to my face, an inch away from my left eye.

My God!!!! I had completely covered up Philadelphia. I had covered up millions of people with my thumb. The thought occurred to me that I was getting hypoxic, so I removed my glove, grabbed my flashlight and looked at my fingernails. They looked normal. If I was lacking oxygen, they would have been purple. The blinker was winking at me.

Well, I suddenly wished I had taken a drink back at the club. The up side was that I didn't have trouble staying awake after that. The down side though, was that I had covered a few million people with my thumb and it took me to another dimension in my mind, a place I would not visit again until the grave marker entered into my life. Years later I would meld these thoughts into one, the sum of which would change my life. I am coming to that.

That innocuous incident made me wonder how important an average individual could be in the whole scope of life. We all live in the small cocoon of our own surroundings and a few friends and places. We are victims of our tiny environments. We stop when the light is red and pay the gas bill when it is due. Strangers move in and out of our lives, only to punctuate the moment with something useful, like a waiter or the paper boy. The human mind somehow wonderfully conjectures that the body in which it resides is important. It is constantly judging others and identifying faults without relating them to itself. In many ways we are but sheep following the dictates of other minds, many of which are not as fruitful as our own. So, is there a deeper meaning to it all? Can we pour all of the non-physical thoughts and happenings into one cohesive boiling pot that will give us something useful? Could some subliminal gene perhaps be the answer to all that we cannot see but know is there?

Later, I laughed at myself and certainly wasn't going to tell anyone about the Philadelphia caper. The Flight Surgeon would have grounded me for sure. But I would remember the feeling it brought and it would later tie into others that would be equally as humbling.

My personal contribution to the Vietnam War was of dubious distinction. I had been shot down once in the south of that country and once again in Laos. My reward for all of that was about a thousand dollars a month in pay, a Silver Star, three Distinguished Flying Crosses, a Bronze Star, sixteen Air Medals and a Purple Heart. And when I boarded the plane that brought me home, two South Vietnamese pilots ran up and handed me a small box, saying, "We want you to have this." It was the Vietnamese Cross of Gallantry, their country's highest medal. Although it was not officially presented, I still value it and the appreciation that came with it. Never mind how important those things were to me at the time, they later added up to a big empty. Was there nothing better to show for that year away from my family and risking my life every day? Maybe so!

Instead of all of those medals, I wish I could have been given a college degree in survival or at least an honorable mention for just having lasted it out. Or maybe when it comes my turn to die, somehow that year could be rebated and tacked on to let me last a little longer. The sense of pride that I felt while serving in that war has since seeped out of me. But I am still alive. What about those whose bones are rotting under the headstones of a thousand wars? Are we forever destined to the same old bloody waste, forever, over and over? Surely there is more out there. But where? Looking back now, I feel as if I was being slowly educated by a larger hand, one that I could not then identify.

I have already said that the whole Vietnam thing was unlikely as far as my participation was concerned. The Philadelphia saga is of no consequence except for the underlying mystic implications that took me years to sort out. Both incidents are important only to me; they have produced something I cherish yet feel inadequate to explain. But I will try.

It is more than sad to me, not just that the French soldiers are dead and buried, but that no one knows where they are or even who they were. No one is crying now that a half a century has passed. The ground knows and the tall grass knows, but they won't tell. And what of the wives and children of those soldiers? Have they gone on to live with a hundred forgotten memories? Sure they have.

So, in my mind, these lines have converged to tell a story that satisfies me in my heart, where only there it really counts. I justify expressing my thoughts here because they have been pounding at me for so long. I certainly can't identify all of the lines that spun the web that forms the latent beliefs that brought me here, but these are some. I borrow now from Omar Khayyam, who died in the first quarter of the twelfth century. His words are some of those that tell the insidious stories the best, stories that have made me think:

> The Moving Finger writes; and, having writ,
>
> Moves on: nor all your Piety nor Wit
>
> Shall lure it back to cancel half a line,
>
> Nor all your tears wash out a word of it.

> Alike for those who for To-day prepare,
>
> And those that after some To-morrow stare,
>
> A Muezzin from the Tower of Darkness cries,
>
> "Fools!" Your Reward is neither Here nor There.

> Strange, is it not? That of the myriads who
>
> Before us pass'd the Door of Darkness through
>
> Not one returns to tell us of the Road,
>
> Which to discover we must travel too.

Those thoughts have so much to say to me. There are others who have said the same thing perhaps less eloquently, but just as meaningfully, such as Andy Warhol, who certainly had his fifteen minutes of fame. Or Shakespeare, in *As You Like It*, who wrote that "All the world's a stage and all the men and women merely players. They have their entrances and their exits, and one man in his time plays many parts."

Okay, Mr. Shakespeare, name just one player or even one part about which you speak! The name may be remembered if it is written, but what of the person? No, each one has faded like the smell of a dying daffodil. No sooner does one depart than another takes its place, again and again, only for the same fate to befall.

Did Shakespeare really say, in other words, that most of us come into this world for a little while, are blessed perhaps, then depart and are soon forgotten by history? Of course he did! And Longfellow, who was born almost 200 years ago, wrote: "Lives of great men all remind us we can make our lives sublime, and departing, leave behind us, footprints in the sands of time."

But what about those of us who are not great men? Are we not somehow entitled to leave a slight footprint... somewhere? Did Lee Harvey Oswald thirst so for a remembrance that nothing else mattered? Or John Wilkes Booth?

Both of them, and a multitude of others, have conveyed the same meaning in vastly different ways and at vastly different times and places. But they all really said the same thing: "Look at me, I'm somebody; please don't forget."

So of course we forgot.

The fun side is that it really doesn't matter who we are if we are someone to ourselves. No one else can think my thoughts, so I am myself only to me. Does that make sense? So, to be important I only need to impress myself. And I can do that if others are positively affected by what they see in me or see me do.

Why do the yellow and purple flowers flourish where no one is there to see? The answer is at last obvious to me. No one has to see what is there. The grass sees, and the trees and rushing waters of the spring creek also see. What has made me think that I had to see the beauty that is there in order to confirm its existence?

We are all here only for the pleasure of others, everything living, only for the pleasure of others. Of course, that's it! That's why the stone marker said "…and smile at a homely girl." It had to be pounded into me! That's why all of Philadelphia was reduced to a thumbnail, to show me that each one is as important as the all, myself no less than any of them, and no more. It seems obvious to me now that we are all temporary statements, like a cut bouquet on the living room table, to make brief comments in passing and maybe cause a smile, then go on to make room for others who will play their parts. Thank you Mr. Shakespeare.

When this realization hit me, at last I knew. If I cannot enrich those with whom I interact each day and cause them to be better for my having passed their view, then I have wasted my turn. That I succeed in this endeavor is not as important as it is for me to make a solid try. For if the try is sincere I have succeeded in whatever failure resulted.

Kiss her on the cheek and whisper something that she will later note in her heart of keepsakes. Open the door for her, not to make her way easier but just to say you care. Be there when she arrives to let her know your time with her is important. Silence can be well understood if she sees an approving look.

So now, at last, at least for me I know. And if no one should ever think of me when I have passed this vale, it will be of no consequence, for I have finally found my way and am at peace with all of it. ∎

Peggy & Forrest
at Fenn Galleries, LTD

BLUE JEANS AND
HUSH PUPPIES AGAIN

When I became a civilian again after twenty years of military life, my retired pay was $12,000 a year, which was adequate to sustain my family of four. We just had to forego a few luxuries like Dr. Peppers and downtown movies. But Lubbock was windy, flat and sedentary, and we could hear the mountains calling. My wife tells the story that when she suggested we move to New Mexico I jumped up and down on my hat, but I don't remember that.

My daughters, Kelly and Zoe, although young, were becoming more and more ambitious for me. The list of people who could afford to dress like they wanted to was very short, and their names weren't on it. So we built an art gallery in Santa Fe and our world started at the bottom again. We learned that a mattress on the floor wasn't bad at all and that we could plaster walls and watch the Cowboys play at the same time. Although our learning curve was flat at first, it was never dull.

The character building lessons of defeat were numerous. One time a lady interviewed me live on Santa Fe Public Radio. Her last question was, "Mr. Fenn, what are the most enjoyable things in life?" I thought for just a second and replied, "A good sneeze, a good scratch and self-pity." I guess it doesn't pay to be so honest, because she quickly broke to a commercial and then disappeared out the side door.

Our gallery soon became a cistern for ideas and opportunities that constantly flowed into it, but I didn't always know if a deal was good or bad. One time a friend came into our gallery with an art dealer from Amarillo. The two of them talked me into giving $5,500 for a black and white oil painting by Gilbert Gaul, who was a Civil War painter with good credentials. I hated to borrow the money, but I did. The scene depicted a man standing on a wooden bridge holding a smoking pistol, with a dead dog at his feet bleeding all over the boards.

Well, over the next few years I tried to sell the painting to everyone I knew and the response was always the same: rolled eyes and an inquiry about the nearest restroom. I finally traded the poor thing to a museum for a small French watercolor, which I happily sold for $1,500. It pictured a bunch of fairies dancing around a rock, if you can believe I'd come to that.

But the result of the whole episode was inordinately profitable for us because it was so educational. I learned about friends, art dealers from Amarillo, Gilbert Gaul, black and white paintings, smoking guns, and dead dogs bleeding on bridges – and I never made many of those mistakes again. Sometimes my memory can have a very long attention span. ∎

Kelly & Zoe

The proprietors

TEACHERS WITH ROPES

Because we really didn't know what we were doing in the art business I tried to browse other stores in town a couple of times a week, just to see what they were doing that might work for us. All I had going for me was some imagination, hard work and a logical mind. One afternoon I walked into the Kachina Gallery on Canyon Road. They sold only kachina dolls that had been made by the Hopi Indians in Arizona. It was surprising to see how much inventory that store had. The dolls were stacked everywhere. They were packed tightly on shelves, jammed in glass cases, and even on the cash register. It was hard to walk through the place, and I immediately noticed several offensive signs that were placed anywhere there was an open spot: "IF YOU TOUCH IT, YOU BOUGHT IT," "YOU ARE RESPONSIBLE FOR YOUR KIDS," and "DO NOT TOUCH." It was outrageously rude of those people to threaten me like that and I suddenly feared for my wallet as well as my life, so I very carefully pulled my shoulders in, put both hands in my pockets and inched for the door. It was a great lesson because that very afternoon we had half-a-dozen little signs strategically placed around our gallery, only ours read, "Please Touch, We Are Responsible."

Our gallery handled what we thought was pretty good art. For that reason we attracted school children from miles around. Teachers loved us because they could take an hour break while I taught their class. And the children loved us because they got an hour break from the teachers. Everyone was happy, including me because I got an hour respite from the tedium of my desk. Even our sales people loved it because they got to loaf for an hour and gossip about me with the teachers while they drank coffee.

After a few visits we had the scenario memorized. The door opened and a teacher walked in and said hello. Then about twenty students came in, single file, each holding fast to a large knot in a long rope. All of the children had their own knots and they couldn't let go under penalty of death. When crossing the street they looked like a giant centipede. Finally a second teacher, who had been at the back of the centipede enforcing discipline, walked in.

The next step in the process was also predictable. After all of the students were inside and counted, and I was introduced, the teachers started for the coffee pot in the back room. They would take about four steps, then the Alpha teacher would turn around

and say in a loud voice, "Now remember what we told you, don't touch anything. DO NOT TOUCH!" The students seemed to enjoy watching the teachers disappear.

"Okay kids, the teachers are gone so now I'm in charge. You may touch anything you want to. And the reason I'm not going to tell you to be careful is because I know you will be, so there is no need to mention it." I always said that. Some of the students giggled when I casually rested my bare arm on the head of a bronze Indian. "Who can tell me what this is?" I would ask. Someone would usually reply, "It's an Indian," another would say, "It's an art," a third might blurt out, "It's a bronze," and a fourth, "It's a sculpture." I always congratulated the class for being so attentive. Then I asked, "Is it hot or is it cold?" Well, that always stumped them, so I'd ask each student to come forward and feel the bronze. They couldn't understand why it was cold to the touch when it was in a warm room. Rather than tell them the bronze felt cold to the touch because their hands were warm, I asked them to consult their parents and write me a letter with the answer. Once I received a nice note from a seven-year-old girl and it was so funny because it said, "My father

thinks you're a fraud." I always thought that's how you should teach a child, hands on and personal, and asking for individual responses when possible.

One time, on a sunny day, a class visited from Espanola. Coincidentally, we were hanging a portrait of George Washington by Gilbert Stuart. It was an important painting and the class could see the $150,000 price on the wall sticker.

Candor requires that I admit to having touched the painting. It happened in my office when no one else was around. The paint I felt with my finger had been applied by Mr. Stuart when the father of our country was sitting just a few feet away. That was exciting to me, and by touching it I could imagine, in some small way, that I also was a part of that company. People collect autographs for the same reason and I feel sorry for those who don't enjoy that depth of imagination.

So we asked the teachers to join us and we sat the kids on the floor in front of the painting. I explained who Washington was, and who the British were, and what the Fourth of July meant, what happened during the Revolutionary War and that Gilbert Stuart had also painted the portrait of George Washington that's on the one-dollar bill.

After passing wash cloths around I asked each student to come forward, one at a time, and touch George Washington (art curators hate me). I explained that when touching a painting, you should not push, or jab, or scrape, or use a fingernail, but ever so gently, just touch the paint and close your eyes. The teachers were horrified at what we were doing but the students loved it and were very serious. Most of them felt George Washington on his nose or chin.

After everyone had taken a turn we went out back and sat on the grass by the pond, because I wanted to ask the students what they had learned. Twelve-year-old boys and girls are a little young to have profound thoughts so I was surprised by the depth of their responses. One girl said that when the Bureau of Engraving designed the one-dollar bill they reversed the image of George Washington for some reason. In the actual portrait he is facing right but on the bill he is facing left.

I loved that comment and explained to the class that art is not meant to be worshiped, but instead, it should be treated as one would treat a friend. Humans possess five senses: sight, smell, touch, taste and hearing. But in most situations where art is concerned, they are allowed to use only their eyes, and many times the object being observed is behind glass. That separation is too impersonal in my view. It's why I wanted the students to touch George Washington. In doing so the painting might provide another dimension, one that is not available to the eyes alone. If that thought is not valid then why would anyone want an original oil painting when a large print of an $80,000,000 Van Gogh can be purchased for $150?

The Alpha teacher had a PhD in art history and she thought she'd use some of it on me, so she asked, in a pointed tone, "What would you do, Mr. Fenn, if one of the youngsters had damaged the painting?" I thought the question was humorous and explained that we would simply have it restored. She looked stunned and her expression insinuated that I should have given her a longer answer. I wanted to tell her that sarcasm is a ploy of the uninformed – but I didn't. Later I inspected the Gilbert Stuart painting under magnification and found no indication that it had been touched.

Several years later, when I was on the plaza enjoying some Häagen Dazs ice cream, a young lady approached me and asked, "You're Mr. Fenn, aren't you? Remember me? I touched George Washington." Once in a while I do something right. ∎

On the way to Taos Mountain

TEA WITH OLGA

Somewhere along the way I learned that my cost could also show a profit. Olga Svoboda was a good example. She lived immediately behind our business in a space that was much too small, even for one person. Her bathtub was just thirty-six inches long and looked crowded in her bathroom. When I offered to move her into a condo and pay all of her housing expenses forever if she would trade me her little casita, she just smiled. She knew I wanted to expand my gallery space and declined, of course. So we laughed and drank red tea.

Then one day she asked me to go to her. When I arrived, her attorney was present. The mood turned somber when she said she was dying of cancer and needed a favor. Her plan was for me to spread her ashes on top of Taos Mountain and in exchange, she would state in her will that I could have her little rooms at their appraised value. She loved the sacred old mountain with its strong ponderosa and aspen groves that blanketed its landscape so completely. She said her father's ashes were there and she wanted to be with him again. The deal was soon struck, so we sipped black tea and nibbled on Oreos.

Olga was a delightful woman with a warm and giving heart. She was also too young to be treated with such disrespect by the ungentle laws of nature and she joked about outrunning the well bug.

She had not seen the mountain from the air so I asked her to fly the ninety miles with me and take one last look. She was fearful of flying and said she would never undertake such an "outrageous adventure." I explained that no one should ever fear crashing because it is only the last inch that counted. That brought a smile but not one of approval. We joked about the irony of my plane wrecking with her ashes on board as being nature's ultimate affront.

Such good-natured repartee continued as the light in her eyes slowly dimmed. Over the weeks and months my little gifts of flowers and bubble gum brought temporary relief but did little to belay the relentless feeling of sadness that permeated our visits. The tea drinking rituals we always enjoyed had somehow become necessities. Although Olga's cancer was insidious and unforgiving by nature, it also allowed time for her to reflect and prepare.

It was bright and sunny when my little plane lifted off and headed north, and I looked forward to performing the promised duty. The billowing clouds seemed to frame the task ahead and with a small window open I enjoyed the ever present aromas of sage and juniper.

My first view of the great mountain brought a shock. The top was covered with snow that I should have known would remain most of the summer. It looked cold and foreboding as I circled, trying to decide what Olga really had wanted. She said "on top of Taos Mountain." That desire seemed unlikely under the circumstances and somewhat aloof from any sober voice of reason. The bitterness of cold remains long after the sweetness of a sentimental moment is forgotten. Surely her father was not way up on top.

I know Olga's spirit was pleased when her white bone fragments flittered through the small window and softly floated down to a place where the chamisa and mountain laurels were blooming, and chipmunks scurried around all year. When my plane and I turned south for home I felt a serene sense of warmth and satisfaction. Olga was at peace at last and I suspected she may be having green tea with her father. Time had taken them apart but it eventually brought them back together. ■

Home from Taos Mountain

NORTH MAIN STREET

THURSDAY 039
1 NOV
1930

Father, sitting and thinking.

The pride of our family,
built in 1930, the year
I was born.

Later, three rooms were added to the back.

FATHER ON THE BANCO

One evening my father was sitting on a banco near the fireplace in my office at the gallery, pretending to read a magazine, while I concluded a transaction with two clients. When the men left he went over to my desk and looked at the paperwork. After studying it for a minute he said, "Son, you've made more money in the last fifteen minutes than my home cost, and it took me twenty years to pay for it." It was a melancholy recollection that suddenly made me feel totally inadequate. When he said he was proud of me it didn't seem to help. He had a master's degree in education and had spent his adult life teaching children, and all I had was a knack for taking care of myself and my family. That still bothers me. When his home mortgage was finally paid, he and my mother went out in the back yard and ceremonially burned the papers. They said it was a religious experience. ■

A good day on the river, I was twelve. What fish we couldn't use
we traded for potatoes and other goods. It's what kept us going
during the war when my father was making $4,000 a year
teaching school in Texas.

FLYWATER

When my parents celebrated their fiftieth wedding anniversary at my sister's house in Bozeman, I thought they were really old, and I think that's funny because my wife and I have been married fifty-seven years and she still looks good and thinks young. We've had a pretty good life together because she's so tolerant, and everyone knows it. She has always said she'd rather switch than fight and I think she's done a lot of switching. But every time we've come to a fork in the road we've taken it together, if you know what I mean. We always used to take separate vacations so she could go visit her mother and talk about me, and I could go visit my father and talk about our favorite fishing holes.

June, July and August in Yellowstone seemed to pass so fast when I was a kid that I often wondered if maybe summer somehow missed the turn there. When the days started to yellow with falling leaves and the mallards began flying south again, I always knew tough times for me were just ahead. Visions of classrooms would loom larger and larger, cutting in to the best times of my life. Over the years so many bits and pieces had to be left behind, and a few mind-expanding experiences were to remain unknown. But as I got older, I realized there were many moments to remember, like the time I sat under a tree on the Madison River and watched the osprey dive

MOUNT HAYNES

WATER HOLE

FATHER

ME

FATHER

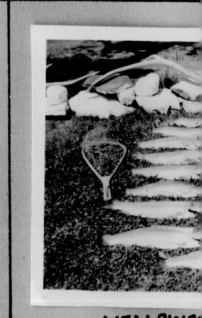

NINE MILE
HOLE

YELLOWS
194
HEBGEN

HIGHWAY HOLE

HIGHWAY HOLE

JUNE

MOM

NE PARK

KE

WATKINS
CREEK

FATHER

for fish as I wrote a note for my wife, who always allowed me the luxury of doing the things I thought were important.

There comes a time (maybe it's an age) when all of us reflect on the happenings that marked our passage through the brakes and thickets of life. Most are conjured up by reverential spirits and are reserved for times when we happen upon the solitude of just ourselves.

A passing mood will bring thoughts of loved ones floating back to dominate a few moments of our time. The reveries are too many to be counted, but each one occupies a far corner of my mind, waiting for another time. I love those things when they do that.

Today, as my thoughts drifted by en route to new ideas to be tried and new experiences to be had, I pulled a long-forgotten book from a shelf. It's called *Flywater*, and is about the great fishing spots in the western part of this country. Several of the wonderful color plates are of places where I fished as a kid under the tutelage of my father, or where I guided others for pay when I was just a young teen.

My secret fishing hole

Those great places, which were personal secrets to me then, are now busy with the flourish of fishermen and women who cast a midge or floating cadis upon those same waters, never knowing I had been there, or even caring yes or no. I always thought that space was mine alone, and many of the memories there bred are even now still so personal that they exclude the intrusion of strangers. How dare they go there?

But I know that as the seasons slowly change and the leaves of life fall and are reborn anew, so do the names of those who wade those waters and chalk the memories once again, this time for themselves. I hope they feel the reverence that I once did and now still do.

How special those hours were, spent watching the waters deepen into cobalt as the flow slowly bent around a bank, or the ripples swirl as a brookie took an unsuspecting mayfly.

Many others who have loved those waters before and after me understand that catching fish is not what it's about. It's the being there, in the tranquility and silence of one's self, or within the gentle call of a friend when he hooks a nice one, or tells you of the moose and calf that just came out of the pines to feed on the water grasses downstream.

The book now occupies a different shelf, closer to my view, for it holds some memories most dear and makes me know that moments such as those are fleet-of-foot indeed and calls to make them all the more. It is well said that "God subtracts from the allotted time of man, those hours spent fishing."

And when my tackle box is closed at last and the cadis hatch is gone, I will rest through all of time and space, pillowed down and scented in, with a smile that comes from remembering the special things that brought me to that final place, one of which was knowing Peggy was there, somewhere, waiting for me. ■

GOLD AND MORE

In my mind I've always been the best in the world at collecting fun things. My career started early with soda pop caps because they were plentiful, free and easy to find: Dr. Pepper, Pepsi, Nehi, Upper 10, Blatz, 7UP, Royal Punch, Coca Cola, Lemon Sour, Orange Crush, Julep Lime and lots more. They all fizzed in my mouth and that's what I liked. I stayed away from diet drinks because I didn't want to lose weight.

My favorite soda was Grapette but the bottle it came in was so small there was almost no room for the drink inside. But I didn't care, I just drank it anyway. One of my rules was that I couldn't collect the cap unless I first drank the pop, but that idea wasn't too good because I didn't have enough nickels to sustain it. When my father grew weary of seeing my great cap collection strewn around the house – like on the floor, on the dresser, on the radio and other places – he formulated a plan that would end my promising career. He went around to all of the gas stations in town that sold soda pops and gathered up hundreds of caps, maybe even thousands. When he gave them to me I quickly lost interest. How could I continue to collect bottle caps when it looked like I already had all that were ever made?

Then I started collecting string, and no kind or color was immune to my desire for it, but most pieces were white. The best saving technique was to tie one end of the new piece of string onto the end of the last one. I knew all of the good tricks, and one was to tie only square knots so they wouldn't slip.

Soon I had a multi-colored ball that got larger and larger with each tie-on. I hoped to tie on at least three strings a day, and after a year or so the ball was so large it couldn't go through my bedroom door.

Then one afternoon when I walked home from school in the rain my string had disappeared. It just wasn't there anymore. I tried to explain to my mother that since the ball couldn't get out of my room it was somewhat difficult for anyone to steal it. She didn't answer, but just kept nodding and looking out of the window. I think she was watching for the postman or something. Even to this day the mystery of what happened to my string ball remains one of the great unsolved crimes in my family.

Over the next fifty years, my eclectic collections grew to excessive proportions: beaded Indian moccasins, fore-edge painted books, weather vanes, ancient Egyptian jewelry, arrowheads, pocket knives and antiques of all kinds.

And then I got a cancer. After a one-hour operation turned into five, my doctor said I had a 20% chance of living three years. Most everyone thought I was going to die, including me. The radiologist only said that I faced an uphill battle. How's that for a mind expanding prognosis?

Lying in bed at three o'clock in the morning, unable to sleep, gave me time to ponder and riffle through my brain looking for answers that I didn't think were there. All sorts of things entered my mind. At age fifty-eight I had spent more than nineteen years asleep, and three of those years were on Monday. Think about that for a minute. Surely that's a design deficiency of some sort.

There was no hero anywhere in me and everything I thought about radiated an aura of misfortune. But nature can be lenient at times, like with Olga, and I figured I had at least a year to live. Strokes and heart attacks don't listen to reason so cancer was probably the best choice if I could have made the selection myself. Before, I had been happy with where my life was, but now, what I seemed to lack in time remaining was conspicuously exceeded by my sudden desire for more of it.

Then one night, after the probability of my fate had finally hit bottom, I got an idea. It had been so much fun building my collection over the decades, why not let others come searching for some of it while I'm still here, and maybe continue looking for it after I'm gone? So I decided to fill a treasure chest with gold and jewels, then secret it – leaving clues on how to find it for any searcher willing to try. It was a perfect match of mind and moment. Ha, I liked the idea but it would take some planning and the clock was ticking. No matter how far away a date is on the calendar, it always seems to arrive sooner in the face of unpleasant situations like mine.

Fortunately, I talked a museum friend into selling me his beautiful cast bronze chest that had three-dimensional female figures on its four sides and on the lid. I know I paid way too much for it but once in a while something comes along that is so special as to discount all logical rules of value. An excited antique scholar said the chest was probably a Romanesque Lock Box that dated to about 1150 AD. He also thought it might have once held a family bible or a Book of Days. Now it could hold my ancient jewelry and solid gold pieces. I was delighted. It was the perfect treasure chest.

I also wanted to include something personal with the treasure because maybe the lucky finder would want to know a little about the foolish person who abandoned such an opulent cache. So I placed a 20,000 word autobiography in the chest. It's in a small glass jar and the lid is covered with wax to protect the contents from moisture. The printed text is so small that a magnifying glass is needed to read the words. I tried to think of everything.

Then I started filling the chest with gold coins, mostly old American eagles and double eagles, along with lots of placer nuggets from Alaska. Two weigh more than a pound each and there are hundreds of smaller ones. Also included are pre-Columbian gold animal figures and ancient Chinese human faces carved from jade. The different objects in the cache are too numerous to mention one by one, but among them are a Spanish 17th century gold ring with a large emerald that was found with a metal detector, and an antique ladies gold dragon coat bracelet that contains 254 rubies, six emeralds, two Ceylon sapphires, and numerous small diamonds.

And with some reluctance I included a small silver bracelet that has twenty-two turquoise disc beads set side-by-side in a row. It fit snug to my arm and I loved it, but its history is what appealed to me the most. Richard Wetherell excavated the beads from a ruin in 1898, and a Navaho silversmith made the bracelet for him the same year. In 1901 Wetherell sold it to Fred Harvey, the hotel magnate. Sixty-four years later I won it playing pool with Byron Harvey, an heir of Fred's.

One of the prizes in my collection, a Tairona and Sinu Indian necklace from Columbia, is also part of the treasure. It contains thirty-nine animal fetishes carved from quartz crystal, carnelian, jadeite and other exotic stones. But special to the necklace are two cast gold objects – one, a jaguar claw and the other, a frog with bulbous eyes and legs cocked as if ready to spring. I held the 2,000-year-old piece of jewelry one last time and could almost feel its ancient power, its supremacy, before I finally lowered it into the

chest and closed the lid. A little of me is also inside the box. There must be a few Indiana Jones types out there, like me, ready to throw a bedroll in the pickup and start searching, with a reasonable chance of discovering a treasure chest containing more than twenty troy pounds of gold. For me, it was always the thrill of the chase. What do you think?

I knew exactly where to hide the chest so it would be difficult to find but not impossible. It's in the mountains somewhere north of Santa Fe. Indecision is the key to flexibility and that's why I waited so long to secret my cache. George Burns was 100 years old when someone asked him how his health was. He replied, "My health's good, it's my age that's killing me." And like Eric Sloane, at age almost-eighty, I figured it was time to act. So I wrote a poem

containing nine clues that if followed precisely, will lead to the end
of my rainbow and the treasure:

As I have gone alone in there
And with my treasures bold,
I can keep my secret where,
And hint of riches new and old.

Begin it where warm waters halt
And take it in the canyon down,
Not far, but too far to walk.
Put in below the home of Brown.

From there it's no place for the meek,
The end is ever drawing nigh;
There'll be no paddle up your creek,
Just heavy loads and water high.

If you've been wise and found the blaze,
Look quickly down, your quest to cease,
But tarry scant with marvel gaze,
Just take the chest and go in peace.

So why is it that I must go
And leave my trove for all to seek?
The answers I already know,
I've done it tired, and now I'm weak.

So hear me all and listen good,
Your effort will be worth the cold.
If you are brave and in the wood
I give you title to the gold.

There are also other subtle clues sprinkled in the stories. It was vital that nobody share my knowledge about the location of the treasure. Two people can keep a secret if one of them is dead. I dreamed the other night that I had been reincarnated as Captain Kidd and went to Gardiner's Island looking for the treasure. It scared me so badly I was jarred awake and don't remember whether I found it or not. ∎

Ring the bell loudly —
    for he who dies with
    over fifty dollars is a failure.

DANCING WITH
THE MILLENNIUM

I've always had a love for history and that's why I like to collect
and talk about old things. Maybe it's because the people who
lived in olden times seem so mysterious to me. I've wondered
what they did when they weren't doing anything. But those who will
be living in the future really arouse my curiosity. Someday, will all of
the land in New Mexico be covered with houses and asphalt? Will
there be no requirement for farmers because everyone will be eating
food pills made with chemicals instead of eating real broccoli and
squash? That might not be all bad.

If those things really come about, what will people do for fresh
air fun? With populations increasing so rapidly maybe there won't
be room for a lot of things we enjoy doing today, like hunting and
hiking and looking across the desert just for the fun of seeing nothing
at all. It seems so sad to me.

Most of those thoughts discourage me because there may not
be any more history in the making like there was in the past. And
worse, what can one person do that might impact life a thousand
years from now? I've given that a lot of thought because little things
can be so important in our lives. For example, do you know how
long a piece of iron is needed to make a horseshoe? You measure
the horse's hoof, front to back, multiply by two and add an inch.

Most people don't know that, but I do because my friend Frank Turley told me. And he told me because he's a blacksmith and I paid him twenty bucks to make me one. I just stood there and watched him bellow the coal to heat the metal. The pinging sound of his pounding hammer against iron and anvil was thrilling to me in a romantic sort of way. It had a certain cadence that was an integral part of the total experience, as were the fumes from his forge that permeated the whole episode. I could have just as easily been watching a smithy in the 7th Cavalry shoe a horse. Those things are important and I'm richer for it.

Anyway, I've never been willing to stand idly by and be part of a forgotten history when I may be able to impact future events. My part will be very small in the big picture but huge to me. "Safe upon the solid rock the ugly houses stand: Come and see my shining palace built upon the sand!"

Imagination is better than knowledge.

Those words from Millay's poem tell my story best and that's where I'm most comfortable. There may be laughter and glee, but because you won't be there when it happens, I'll tell you of my secret plan.

On many occasions at night, while my wife was watching "Dancing With the Stars," I was making wax bells and writing words on them in elevated letters. The later bronze castings of the bells are exactly like the wax originals I took to the foundry. Bronze is a non-ferrous metal, meaning it won't rust or deteriorate in any way. One must pound it with a sledgehammer, or melt it down in order to change its shape. All of my bells were cast in that material so I could bury them. Each one is signed and dated or there would be no point to the madness. Some of the bells have clankers that I made from large copper nails taken from 17th century Spanish galleons. Skippy's son, Crayton Fenn, is a professional deep sea diver. He gave the nails to me.

If you should ever think of me,
a thousand years from now,
please ring my bell so I will know.

I buried those bells about three feet deep so a metal detector can't find them. Some may be on land owned by the American people but tended by the Bureau of Land Management. Other bells have words that say:

GOD WILL FORGIVE ME, THAT'S WHAT HE DOES.

IMAGINATION IS MORE IMPORTANT
THAN KNOWLEGE.

IT DOESN'T MATTER WHO YOU ARE,
IT ONLY MATTERS WHO THEY THINK YOU ARE.

There are others but these illustrate my point if not my logic. Hopefully no one will happen upon a bell for many years – around 1,000 would be perfect. The Rosetta Stone was undiscovered for 2,000 years and don't you just know the guy who carved it is proud?

I'm also burying bronze jars for the same reason, about eight in all. My friend, Tommy Hicks, who owns Shidoni Foundry, didn't know how to cast jars with screw-on lids, so I had to teach him. It's a secret technique that I discovered when I ran my own art foundry many years ago. The same autobiography that's in the treasure chest also is in the jars, which are decorated mostly with dragonfly or frog designs. Frogs are kind of my specialty because I like to fabricate long legs and buggy eyes in the soft wax.

So now I have to wonder about myself doing all of those things that others must think are so foolish. Is there any wisdom in trying to cause momentary excitement in some future millennium? I'm not sure I can even define history in those terms. And what if no one ever discovers my art? Will my time have been wasted? I guess the rewards have been in doing it, and the enjoyment that comes with dreaming about what might happen someday. No matter. It was more fun to run the risk of being foolish than to watch "Dancing With the Stars." ∎

Imagination is more important than knowlege.

My team, Kelly, Peggy & Zoe

ODE TO PEGGY JEAN

Cancer is a terrible word. No pleasant thoughts are conjured up when it's spoken and pulse rates quicken for no reason other than to hear it said. The disease it defines represents nature in its most repellent form.

At age fifty-eight, invasive cells came into my body and took a kidney. That was bad enough, but the mental diagnosis I gave myself was worse. I waited too long; my inferior vena cava was imbedded with a hateful, chewing malignancy. My surgeon, Dr. Taylor Floyd, did more than could be demanded from any earthly being. His genius gave me hope, however faint. My life was on hold as chemotherapy and radiation treatments took additional tolls on my spirit and my body.

Then out of nowhere came a family charge led by my wife, who refused to accept any abstract judgments that ran contrary to my total recovery. No saint could match her faith. She and my daughters, Kelly and Zoe, provided warm comfort and encouraged me to fight the despair that so dampened my slowly passing hours. Through the many bedridden weeks they were with me, and by me, and for me. They nursed my weakened confidence all along the mucky trail that I thought was disappearing into the black abyss of medical odds. Peggy sensed so completely the vital consequence of my struggle that I believe she frightened away any remnants of the disease. They must have fled in dreadful horror in the face of her focused passion and unshakable determination. My team had saved my life.

ODE TO PEGGY JEAN

Today I looked up in the sky
   And saw a sparrow on the fly.
What ancient secrets does he know?
   Why am I here and cannot go?

Today I looked up in the sky
   And saw a raven flying by.
He seemed so focused on his way
   So tell me now why I must stay.

Today I looked up in the sky
   And saw my shadow floating by.
It seemed so strange - I wondered why.
   And now it's gone, but where am I?

Today I looked up in the sky
   And saw that I shall never die.
Forget the pain and harm you see,
   My loving wife looks after me.

I recovered after having planned my future up to one detail short of the final bier. I had even plotted to have my bones rest forever, in silent repose, beside the treasure chest. If I had to go I wanted to do it on my own terms as my father had done two years earlier, with no hospital bed to offer a temporary postponement. It was important to me that I dared to be myself. Today I live my life with renewed meaning, but always with the awareness that some insidious strain might again sneak into my body. I hope my age has pushed me far enough ahead so as to discourage even a most persistent chase. ■

My Father — born 1903

EPILOGUE

Now as I look back with the vision of seventy-nine years to lean against, I wonder what I've learned – and several things come to mind. I've learned that having enough money is much better than having a lot of money, because casual cash propagates idle fingers. And I've learned that anguish wrought by misdeeds made in later life comes in larger doses than with misdeeds made in adolescence. Only an experience can teach thoroughly and with a speed that is not always available in the classroom. Embarrassing incidents educate the best and the fastest and can come with a lasting sting. And what I've learned that's most important is that both countries and people should know enough to just leave other folks alone and do a better job of protecting our planet.

My father was a dedicated educator and he went about his day as adroitly as any of the best in his time. At age eighty-three he took his own life in order to defeat a cancer that had chewed on his pancreas for too long. He was not going to let it beat him. I admired him for making such a sensible and brave decision. His funeral was held at the large First Baptist Church in Temple, Texas, and he had it all planned: who the pastor would be, who would sing which songs, what kind of flowers he wanted and who should sit where.

The sanctuary was filled and maybe a hundred friends were standing outside, hoping to hear the words that were being spoken with such passion and eloquence. The preacher said that it was probably the largest crowd he had ever seen at a funeral. It was a testimonial to who my father was and how his life affected nearly all humans with whom he mingled. I can't remember how many times, when walking down the street with my father, a man would come up to us and say, "You're Mr. Fenn, aren't you? You gave me a few spankings when I was in junior high." My father would always ask, "Well, did you deserve the spankings?" The man would grin, "Well, yes." "Then I'm glad I gave you the lickings because you look like a fine man now." That's what my father always said. He had it down. Most likely the other guy would mumble something like, "I just wanted to shake your hand," and they both would smile as life continued.

His name was William Marvin Fenn. He molded so many lives and made such a huge and far-reaching impact on the local society that I was sure everyone would remember him forever. Yet when I looked him up on Google I discovered that he's buried

alongside my mother in row 4 of block 23 at the Hillcrest Cemetery, and that's about it. Maybe history doesn't want us to remember everything we've learned, and that's why the grass grows so tall over a French soldier's headstone in Vietnam.

Now I feel that my father is sitting on the edge of a cloud somewhere watching. If he knows everything about me he's pretty busy lighting candles, some of them on both ends. But I hope he knows that I've been sometimes guilty only by innuendo, and that's why I wrote my epitaph with such profundity:

I wish I could have lived to do, the things I was attributed to.

No time spent in thought is wasted and nothing is too small to know, so one should not let knowing a little bit be a substitute for learning more. The aspirations of youth grow weak where they languish on the shelves of patience, and some of the things I've enjoyed the most in my life have come from the smallest voices. That a butterfly is really a "flutterby" is one example.

In writing this memoir I've rediscovered things about myself I thought were long forgotten. It would be nice to start life over and do it all again. I'd change so much, but only for the sake of new adventures. And that's why I think youth should always be wasted on the young. But what do I know?

The past will always be contradictory when told by one person at a time. I feel my life has been a rough draft of the place just ahead where the past will come alive again and all of my experiences and friends through the years will meet with me at the great banquet table of history. Then there will be no past. ■

ΩΩ

COLOPHON

THE THRILL OF THE CHASE
A MEMOIR
2010

CREATIVE DIRECTION
Bruno Advertising+Design, Santa Fe, New Mexico

DESIGN AND PRODUCTION
S Caldwell Design, Santa Fe, New Mexico

BODY TEXT
Adobe Garamond

CAPTION TEXT
Marydale

PAPER STOCK
Platinum Silk 100 lb. text

PRINTED BY
Starline Printing, Albuquerque, New Mexico

BOUND BY
Roswell Bookbinding, Phoenix, Arizona